SIMPLY
ECONOMICS

DK LONDON

Senior Editor Kathryn Hennessy
Designer Daksheeta Pattni
Editors Elizabeth Dowsett, Lydia Halliday,
Andrea Page, Victoria Pyke
Illustrators Phil Gamble, Vanessa Hamilton
Managing Editor Gareth Jones
Senior Managing Art Editor Lee Griffiths
Production Editor Jacqueline Street-Elkayam
Senior Production Controller Rachel Ng
Jacket Design Development Manager
Sophia M.T.T.
Jacket Designer Akiko Kato
Associate Publishing Director Liz Wheeler
Art Director Karen Self
Publishing Director Jonathan Metcalf

First published in Great Britain in 2022 by
Dorling Kindersley Limited
20 Vauxhall Bridge Road,
London SW1V 2SA

The authorised representative in the EEA is
Dorling Kindersley Verlag GmbH. Arnulfstr. 124,
80636 Munich, Germany

Copyright © 2022 Dorling Kindersley Limited
A Penguin Random House Company
10 9 8 7 6 5 4 3 2
009–322093–Nov/2022

A CIP catalogue record for this book
is available from the British Library.
ISBN: 978-0-2414-7131-9

Printed and bound in China

www.dk.com

MIX
Paper | Supporting
responsible forestry
FSC™ C018179

This book was
made with Forest
Stewardship
Council™ certified
paper – one small
step in DK's
commitment to a
sustainable future.
**Learn more at
www.dk.com/uk/
information/
sustainability**

CONSULTANT

Peter Antonioni is a lecturer in the
Department of Management Science and
Innovation at UCL, where he teaches the
economics of technology and information
sectors. He holds a BA in Philosophy,
Politics, and Economics from Oxford
University and an MSc in Economics
from Birkbeck College, London. He is
also a regular panellist at the Kilkenomics
festival of economics and comedy.

CONTRIBUTORS

John Farndon is an award-winning
author who has written over 1,000
books, including overviews of the
booming economies of China and India,
and contributed to many DK titles,
including *The Economics Book* and
How Business Works.

Shari Last is an author and editor of
bestselling reference books and has
contributed to numerous DK titles.

Philip Parker is a critically acclaimed
author and award-winning editor who has
contributed to many DK books. He holds
a Diploma in International Relations from
Johns Hopkins University and is the
author of *History of World Trade in Maps*.

CONTENTS

ECONOMIES
IN **ACTION**

CHOICES AND CONSEQUENCES

THE ROLE OF MARKETS

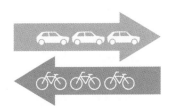

INTERNATIONAL TRADE

UNDERSTANDING FINANCE

WHAT IS ECONOMICS?

Economics is the study of production and distribution. Economists seek to understand how goods and services are produced and who consumes them. They then use this understanding to advise society on how to get the highest value from production using the fewest resources. Economics involves looking at both the small picture – how individuals and households consume and make decisions, and the very large picture – how countries can help their economies to grow and what causes an economy to go into decline.

One focus of economics is on how markets shape decisions about production and distribution. Economists use a range of tools to analyse market behaviour. They might look at costs and prices, for instance, or how different ways of organizing markets can have different outcomes. They are also interested in how markets might fail to produce the best outcomes and how those failures can be avoided or corrected.

Economists use models – mathematical or conceptual maps of a situation – to simulate and understand real-world problems. These models remove or simplify some of the details of reality in order to gain a better understanding of how a market, or even a country, changes as individuals or institutions make different choices. This kind of economic analysis leads to two types of conclusion: positive statements (accounts of how the world is; for example, "excess supply leads to falling prices") and normative statements (accounts of how things "should" be; for instance, "a government should choose a different monetary policy"). It is not always easy to differentiate between which statements can and cannot be verified, so economists look carefully at conclusions about what "should" be done and try to tease out the possible consequences of different courses of action.

FOUNDA
OF ECON

TIONS
OMICS

Modern economics rests on a set of foundational ideas. Core to these is the concept of scarcity. Because all resources are scarce (land, time, money, etc.), nobody is able to have or do everything. Therefore, people must make decisions about how to meet their potentially limitless wants and needs. The key principles of economics build on the role of scarcity in decision-making, and they are the basis for the models that economists use to analyse and draw conclusions about complex real-world behaviour. Some of these conclusions differ from economist to economist, depending on their perspectives, and divergent schools of economic thought have developed as a result.

> **"The most valuable of all capital is that invested in human beings..."**
> Alfred Marshall

Microeconomists look at the individual pieces of an economy, such as a particular household or business, and how they interact and make decisions in a competitive market.

THINKING SMALL

Microeconomics is the study of how the individuals and businesses that make up an economy behave. Its focus is on "economic agents" – individual people, consumers, households, or businesses – and the individual economic choices they make. Microeconomics is underpinned by the assumption that each agent is in competition with the others to get the maximum utility – that is to say, the best outcome for themselves. Economic agents are both producers and consumers. As they interact in competitive markets, producers create supply and consumers create demand which, in turn, determines both prices and output.

THINKING BIG

Macroeconomics is the study of the economy of an entire nation or region – or even the whole world. Macroeconomists may look at unemployment and interest rates, or inflation, as seen in the Consumer Price Index (CPI; see p.55). They also study economic growth and decline, of which Gross Domestic Product (GDP) is one measure (see p.38). Governments look to macroeconomics to find ways to promote growth or limit recessions. The effects of macroeconomic factors such as unemployment and inflation on an economy can have an impact on everyone, everywhere.

BIG PICTURE
Macroeconomics is concerned with the economy of a whole region, measuring factors such as overall growth, unemployment, or price changes.

Ecological economics

Founded in the 1980s, this field develops techniques to value biodiversity and the environment and to cost environmental harms.

Schumpeterian economics

In the first half of the 20th century, Joseph Schumpeter highlighted the role of entrepreneurship, innovation (see p.110), and creative destruction (see p.111) in the way economies evolve.

Keynesian economics

John Maynard Keynes's macroeconomic ideas from the 1930s emphasize the positive impact of government investment and intervention, in part because prices and wages do not adjust easily to sudden changes in market conditions.

Classical economics

Classical economists emphasize the role of markets in coordinating production and distribution. The school of thought began with the ideas of Adam Smith in the late 18th century (see p.24).

SCHOOLS OF THOUGHT

While economists all consider the same complex questions about the production and distribution of resources in society, they come with their own perspectives and reach different conclusions. Over time, multiple schools of economics have emerged, influenced by – and sometimes contradicting – those that have gone before. The schools provide tools for economic analysis, sometimes very differently from each other. Each tends to emphasize separate features of the economy in their studies.

Well-being and Caring economics

These early 21st-century approaches reject simple utility maximization (see p.71) and try to place decisions in the context of social psychology.

Complexity economics

Increasingly popular, the new approach of complex systems uses maths and insights from physics and biology to model economies as large, interconnected systems.

Behavioural economics

Emerging after World War II, this school draws on elements from economics and psychology. It uses scientific experiments to show biases in decision-making and how people differ from the classical rationality model (see p.14).

Austrian economics

From the late 19th century, the Austrian school emphasizes entrepreneurship and the ability of the free market to coordinate production. It prefers not to use mathematical analysis.

Marxist economics

In the late 19th century, Karl Marx believed capitalism was destined to fail, and he described the class struggle between owners (capital) and workers (labour). His ideas influenced socialism and many real-world economies.

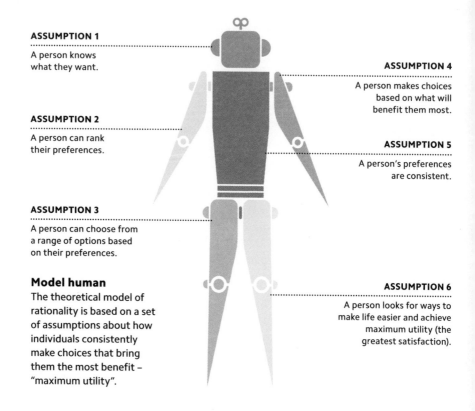

ASSUMPTION 1

A person knows
what they want.

ASSUMPTION 2

A person can rank
their preferences.

ASSUMPTION 3

A person can choose from
a range of options based
on their preferences.

Model human

The theoretical model of
rationality is based on a set
of assumptions about how
individuals consistently
make choices that bring
them the most benefit –
"maximum utility".

ASSUMPTION 4

A person makes choices
based on what will
benefit them most.

ASSUMPTION 5

A person's preferences
are consistent.

ASSUMPTION 6

A person looks for ways to
make life easier and achieve
maximum utility (the
greatest satisfaction).

RATIONALITY

Since economists generally have little information
about what kind of individuals people are, they use a set
of rules called "rationality", which allows them to model
human decision-making based on the fewest assumptions
possible. Rationality presents people as being able to
choose the highest level of utility (what brings them the
greatest satisfaction) given their constraints, and being
consistent in doing so. In real life, of course, people
do not always behave in such a predictable way.

ECONOMICS

PSYCHOLOGY

CULTURE

SOCIAL ISSUES

RATIONAL BEINGS

Classical economic models suggest that people weigh up the costs and benefits of decisions to maximize their gain.

IRRATIONAL BEINGS

Emotions and other factors can influence decision-making so people do not always act logically in their self-interest.

PEOPLE AREN'T ALWAYS RATIONAL

Many economic theories are based on the assumption that humans behave rationally and only to benefit themselves. Behavioural economics argues that human psychology affects every decision, so behaviour is not always rational. Consumer decisions are affected by many factors, including emotion, unconscious bias, and cultural influences. Two brands might sell exactly the same product, but a consumer may pay more for their preferred one. Businesses often use behavioural economics to inform their strategies.

> "Marginal costs and marginal benefits are what really matter for the efficiency of an economy."
> Tim Harford

Economic decisions are not taken all at once but in increments.

ONE STEP AT A TIME

Marginalism is the economic insight that decisions about buying, selling, production, and consumption are made in increments rather than all at once. Economists refer to these increments as being "at the margin" – in other words, what matters is the next little decision. The marginal value of a product or service is the amount someone is willing to pay for an additional unit of it at any given moment. The marginal cost of a product or service is not the total production cost divided by the number of units, but the cost of producing one extra unit.

MEASURING VALUE

Utility is the term given to the sense of satisfaction felt from buying a product or service. A consumer values the utility of a product, not the product itself. It includes not just the practical benefits of a purchase, but also how a consumer feels about it. Utility cannot be measured directly, but price can be an indicator of it. For example, a price rise reduces a consumer's satisfaction, so they may change what they buy to maximize their utility.

Marginal utility describes what a consumer gains from one extra unit of a product or service.

Diminishing marginal utility
Sometimes utility falls as more of a product is consumed. For example, the utility a person gets from their first biscuit of the day is likely to be greater than what they gain from their tenth.

SCARCITY

Scarcity is the gap between unlimited wants and limited resources. As long as there is not enough of something to satisfy everyone's needs and wants, there is scarcity. Because resources such as land, time, and money are scarce, choices have to be made as to how to allocate them, and this is the basis of all economics. If there were unlimited resources, there would be no need to make choices. Scarcity of something that is in high demand, such as gold or expert knowledge, pushes up the price of that product or service.

> "Economics brings into view that conflict of choice..."
> Lionel Robbins

UNLIMITED WANTS

LIMITED RESOURCES

ECONOMIC "INGREDIENTS"

Goods and services are produced using four kinds of resource, or "factors of production" – land, labour, capital, and enterprise. "Land" includes both farming land and all the raw materials that come from the earth, such as oil and metal ores. "Labour" is the work that individuals put in to create a product or provide a service. "Capital" refers not to money in this context, but to the tools or equipment used in production. These factors are brought together by "enterprise" – the ability and drive to innovate and make a profit.

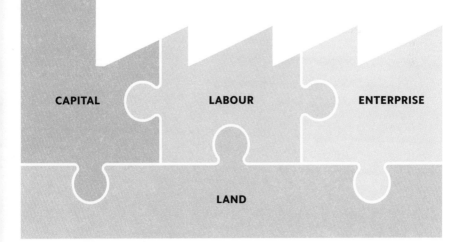

Building blocks of the economy
These four resources (or inputs) are needed to create goods or services (outputs) for economic profit.

WHAT IS MONEY?

Money has various uses. It is a "medium of exchange" between a buyer and a seller, meaning that it can be swapped for something else. Its value is based not on the materials it is made from, but on what you can exchange it for. Money is a "unit of account" – a universally accepted way of measuring and comparing the worth of different items. It can also be used to value a debt, as a "standard of deferred payment", which allows a buyer to acquire an asset now but pay later. Lastly, because it is not perishable, it can be saved for the future as a "store of value".

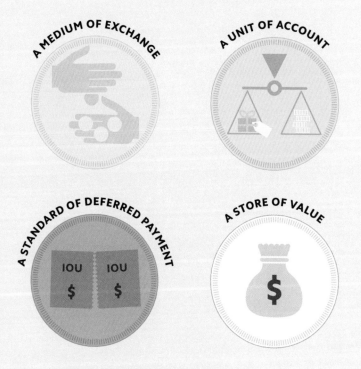

A MEDIUM OF EXCHANGE

A UNIT OF ACCOUNT

A STANDARD OF DEFERRED PAYMENT

IOU $

IOU $

A STORE OF VALUE

$

THE KEY TO CAPITALISM

RIGHT TO USE THE PROPERTY OWNED

RIGHT TO EARN AN INCOME FROM IT

RIGHT TO TRANSFER IT TO OTHERS

RIGHT TO ENFORCE PROPERTY RIGHTS

Property rights are at the heart of the economic system of capitalism, which emerged in the 17th and 18th centuries. In a capitalist economy, "property", such as businesses, is owned by individuals or groups, rather than by the state. These private owners can seek to increase the value of their property and gain a profit from it, which they can then invest or take as income. The state acts as a guarantor, passing laws safeguarding private ownership of property and its associated rights – including the right to sell. If it is clear to everyone who owns what, it is more likely that transactions will take place, and the market will be more efficient.

ECONOMIC MEASUREMENTS

There are two kinds of measurements of interest
to economists: stocks and flows. Stocks are the total
quantity of wealth (goods, assets, funds, etc.) that is held
and ready to use. Flows are the movement of that wealth
in and out over a particular period of time. The balance
between inflows (income) and outflows (spending)
determines whether stock is increasing or decreasing.

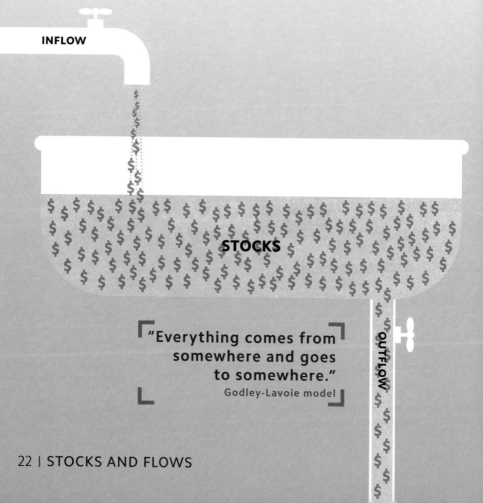

INFLOW

STOCKS

"Everything comes from
somewhere and goes
to somewhere."
Godley-Lavoie model

OUTFLOW

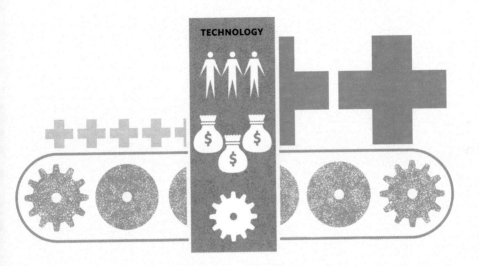

TECHNOLOGY

In economics, technology is the term for anything that makes it possible to produce more or better goods and services at a lower cost. It refers to how inputs are combined to create an output. There are two main types of input: capital (money or other assets such as machinery) and labour (human workers and their skills). When a company applies a technology, it blends inputs to maximize the output for the minimum cost. The "technical rate of substitution" of a technology expresses how much one input (such as labour) would have to be changed in order to maintain productivity if another input (such as machinery) changed.

THE FREE MARKET

In the 18th century, Adam Smith proposed that a market thrives best when left alone. He argued that when individuals act in their own interest within a free market, it benefits everyone – albeit unintentionally. Each market exchange (the interaction between buyers and sellers) signals what consumers want (demand), what products or services are available (supply), and their value (price). As people make exchanges based on self-interest, supply, demand, and prices move up and down in relation to each other, as if guided by an invisible hand. Everyone gets what they want, keeping the market in a balanced state of "equilibrium".

SUPPLY

DEMAND

Balancing act
In Smith's view, allowing the "invisible hand" of free exchange to guide the market forces of supply and demand is more effective than government regulations and interventions.

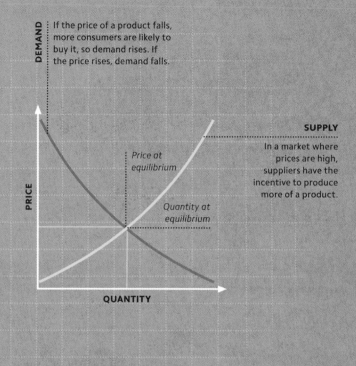

DEMAND

If the price of a product falls, more consumers are likely to buy it, so demand rises. If the price rises, demand falls.

SUPPLY

In a market where prices are high, suppliers have the incentive to produce more of a product.

Price at equilibrium

Quantity at equilibrium

PRICE

QUANTITY

GIVE AND TAKE

In microeconomics (see p.10), the term "supply and demand" refers to the relationship between the quantity of goods and services on sale and the quantity consumers want to buy. The pricing of goods is determined by the interaction between supply and demand in the market. As prices escalate, demand falls and supply builds up. As supply rises and demand falls, prices may fall. Where demand and supply match, the market will be in equilibrium. The price paid at this point of balance is called the "equilibrium price".

TYPES OF MARKET

How a society decides what is produced, how it is produced, and who benefits from it depends on its type of market system. A free market economy operates without rules or regulations, relying purely on supply and demand (see p.25) and the drive for profits. In contrast, a centrally planned economy is completely controlled by the state. Most markets today are mixed economies in which the government enacts some policies and controls parts of the economy (such as healthcare), but the rest is left alone. Some countries, such as China, have moved from a planned economy to a mixed economy that still retains some socialist values and a significant number of state-owned enterprises.

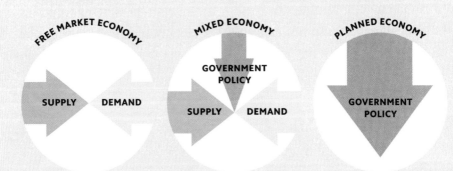

FREE MARKET ECONOMY

SUPPLY DEMAND

MIXED ECONOMY

GOVERNMENT POLICY

SUPPLY DEMAND

PLANNED ECONOMY

GOVERNMENT POLICY

Trade is based on personal profit maximization, with no regulations or limits. While there are no fully free economies in the world, some have less state intervention than others.

There is usually a public and private sector. Private innovation, wealth, and capitalism are encouraged, but governments may introduce limits, sanctions, or taxes.

The government controls all aspects of production as part of a centralized plan, including setting prices. Sometimes all property is held communally, not privately.

WIN-WIN TRADES

Gains to trade occur when two or more parties trade freely in goods and services. Both parties benefit from the voluntary exchange. The amount of gain can be calculated by the community surplus (see p.104). When a market is in equilibrium, there will be no unexploited gains to trade and all parties receive the maximum benefit. One example of gains to trade is in international trade: countries benefit from lowering any barriers to trade and specializing in areas where they have comparative advantage (see p.127).

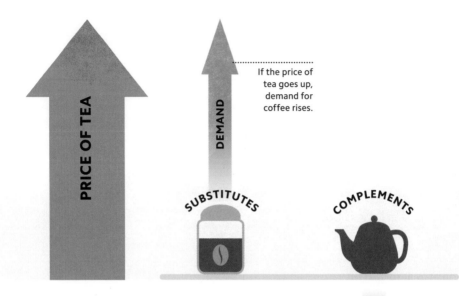

PRICE OF TEA

DEMAND

SUBSTITUTES

If the price of tea goes up, demand for coffee rises.

COMPLEMENTS

DEMAND

If the price of tea goes up, demand for teapots goes down.

FRIEND OR FOE

Substitute goods are items used for the same (or similar) purpose, such as tea and coffee. A consumer will often choose one or the other, so the goods compete with each other. Complementary goods, on the other hand, are items that are used together – for example, tea and teapots. Demand for a certain good will affect the demand for both its substitute and complementary goods. If, say, the price of tea goes up, demand for tea will go down. This will also lower demand for its complements (such as teapots), but increase demand for its substitutes (such as coffee).

MONEY AND CHOICE

Goods are tangible items – both physical and digital – that can be purchased. As income increases, the demand for various goods changes. "Normal" goods, such as books, food, and household items, come to be in higher demand (with an income elasticity of between 0 and 1; see p.31), while more affordable "inferior" goods, such as second-hand clothes or generic supermarket brands, are in lower demand (with an income elasticity of less than 0). "Luxury" goods, such as sports cars, are a type of normal good because demand for them also increases with income – but their income elasticity is greater than 1.

INCOME RISES

Luxury
As income rises, the demand for luxury goods goes up, and consumers spend a larger part of their income on them.

Normal
Consumers spend more as their income increases, so the demand for normal goods goes up.

Inferior
As income goes up, the demand for inferior goods falls because consumers are switching to normal goods.

CHANGE BREEDS CHANGE

Own-price elasticity
This measures how strongly the supply or demand of an item varies in response to a change in price. Inelastic demand shows little or no change; elastic demand shows strong change.

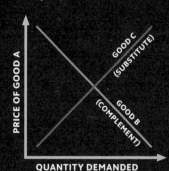

INELASTIC DEMAND

PRICE

ELASTIC DEMAND

QUANTITY DEMANDED

Cross-price elasticity
This measures the effect on demand for one good when the price of another changes. If the price rises, demand for a substitute will rise, but demand for a complement will fall (see p.29).

PRICE OF GOOD A

GOOD C (SUBSTITUTE)

GOOD B (COMPLEMENT)

QUANTITY DEMANDED OF GOOD B OR GOOD C

Elasticity is a measure of the sensitivity of one economic factor, such as demand, to change in others, such as price or income. Demand can be "elastic" or "inelastic", depending on how much it is affected by the change. For example, insulin is said to be an inelastic good because demand remains the same if the price goes up. Leisure trips, on the other hand, are highly elastic, with demand falling quickly as prices rise. Economists measure this responsiveness using a "coefficient of elasticity" – a coefficient above 1.0 is very elastic; a coefficient of 0 is completely inelastic. There are four main types of elasticity: own-price, cross-price, income, and substitution.

Income elasticity

This measures the change in demand for goods in response to a change in a person's income. Inelastic demand shows a good is a necessity; elastic demand shows it is a luxury.

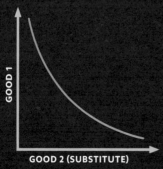

Elasticity of substitution

This is a measure of how easily a good can be substituted. The easier it is for consumers to switch, the more elastic demand will be.

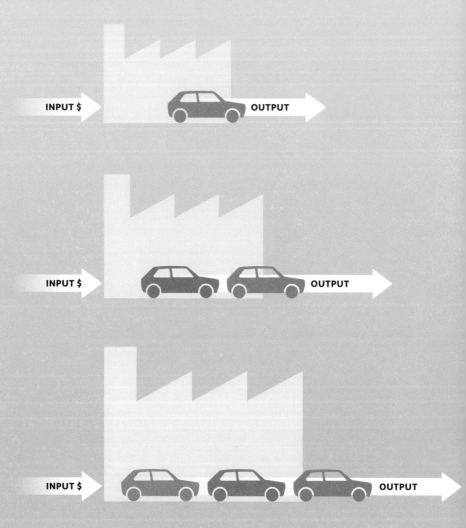

Economy of scale
Some fixed costs must be paid regardless of
the output, so producing more of something
brings the price per unit down. The bigger
the factory, the lower the average cost.

Economy of scope
Increasing the scope (range of products) can bring costs down, as long as the same resources can be used to make each product. A car, lorry, and tractor may all have the same sort of engine.

> "... economy of skill, economy of specialized machinery, and economy of materials."
> Alfred Marshall

EXPAND AND DIVERSIFY

Economies of scale and economies of scope are ways in which businesses can lower their costs and gain a competitive advantage over their rivals through growth or diversification. Economies of scale arise where a business can make items more cheaply by producing them in a greater number. For example, a carmaker may find it costs $500,000 to make five cars ($100,000 each), but just $100m to make 10,000 cars ($10,000 each). Economies of scope occur where a business can make a wider variety of products using common "inputs" (resources such as labour, components, or equipment). A carmaker might, for example, benefit if it also built other types of vehicles from common components.

UNLOCKING POTENTIAL

In economics, the terms "short run" and "long run" do not refer to periods of time, but to how possible it is to change the factors that affect production. The short run means that, for now, at least one factor of production is fixed and cannot be changed. For instance, a business may be able to boost production by asking workers to work overtime, but its capacity is limited by the size of the factory. In the long run, all factors of production can be changed – for example, another factory could be built or a more efficient production process could be developed.

SHORT RUN

In the short run, at least one factor of production is locked and cannot be changed – for example, available capital.

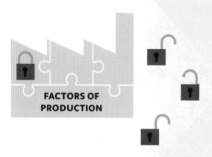

FACTORS OF PRODUCTION

FACTORS OF PRODUCTION

In the long run, all factors of production can be unlocked and changed in response to a changing market.

LONG RUN

Specialization
Splitting work into specialized
tasks increases productivity.
Goods can be mass-produced if
each worker on a production line
performs a different function.

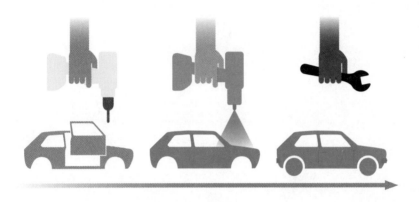

DIVISION OF LABOUR

Division of labour refers to who does which job. In the 18th
century, Adam Smith argued that production would be more
efficient if individual workers were to specialize in, and focus on,
a particular task, rather than doing everything. This would allow
them to develop special skills, as well as to work faster and to
a better standard. Smith saw specialization as the engine of
economic growth. Today, labour division is the norm in most
businesses, and even works on a global scale. But some
economists have argued that it creates hierarchies both
in the workplace and society at large – for instance,
between skilled and unskilled workers.

ECONO
INACT

MIES
ION

Economies are made up of individual decisions – from small ones, like which type of canned drink to buy, to big ones, like how much tax the government should levy on the population. The big decisions are the ones that make the news headlines, and understanding the core economic concepts that inform those decisions – from taxation and inflation to interest rates and unemployment – helps us to see how they affect everyday life. Economists also consider the core concepts when analysing economies in order to try to anticipate what the impact of different policies might be; for example, interventions by governments (fiscal policy) or central banks (monetary policy).

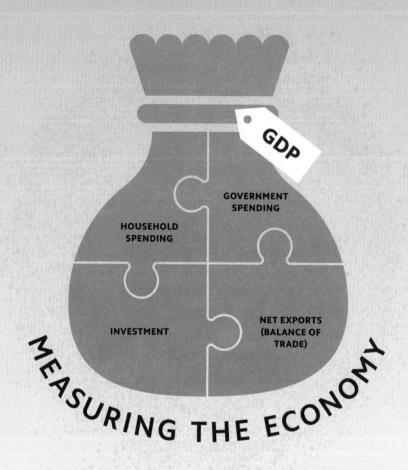

GDP

GOVERNMENT
SPENDING

HOUSEHOLD
SPENDING

INVESTMENT

NET EXPORTS
(BALANCE OF
TRADE)

MEASURING THE ECONOMY

Gross Domestic Product (GDP) is a measure of a country's economic value and health over a period of time. It can be used to monitor the growth of an economy, compare its size with that of other countries, or measure a country's standard of living (GDP per capita/person). GDP is adjusted in different ways – for instance, to account for inflation – but essentially it is the sum of consumer spending on domestic goods and services, government spending, private domestic investment (money spent by businesses), and the balance of foreign trade (see p.124).

OUTPUT VS SPENDING

Aggregate supply and aggregate demand are macroeconomic
(see p.11) terms for the total supply of and the total demand
for goods and services in an economy at a given time.
Aggregate supply is everything the economy produces
and sells – also known as Gross Domestic Product (GDP;
see opposite). Aggregate demand is the total spending on
domestic goods and services. The balance between them
is reflected in the relationship between output and price.

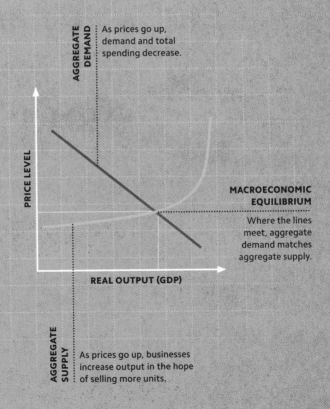

AGGREGATE DEMAND
As prices go up,
demand and total
spending decrease.

PRICE LEVEL

MACROECONOMIC EQUILIBRIUM
Where the lines
meet, aggregate
demand matches
aggregate supply.

REAL OUTPUT (GDP)

AGGREGATE SUPPLY
As prices go up, businesses
increase output in the hope
of selling more units.

KEEPING MARKETS ON TRACK

In a free market economy, theoretically all decisions would be made by private firms and individuals, with no government involvement. However, in practice, there is no country in the world where the government does not play an economic role, however lightly. For example, the state preserves property rights, raises taxes, provides public goods and services, and regulates markets. Most also attempt to steer the economy using fiscal (see p.44) and monetary policies (see pp.58–59).

Regulator
Passes protective laws – for example, around minimum wages, health and safety, maximum working hours, and limits on pollution.

Investor
Funds services not provided by the market, such as investing in an educated workforce and building essential infrastructure.

Economic actor
Sets fiscal and monetary policy in a bid to ease the country through the economic cycle's booms and recessions.

Controller of social resources
Manages resources essential to the normal functioning of society and people's well being, such as water and open spaces.

Guarantor of free and fair competition
Helps the market run smoothly – for example, by regulating against monopolies (see p.96).

Preserver of law and order
Upholds property rights and law and order – vital to the functioning of the market – through the courts, policing, and national defence.

BALANCING PUBLIC FINANCES

The public sector provides public goods (see p.101) and services (see p.43), run by the government. It receives most of its income from taxes, but it can also charge for services, issue fines, and collect returns on any investments (rent, dividends, and interest). To raise more, it can borrow from investors like pension funds by selling government bonds, but it must pay interest on this debt.

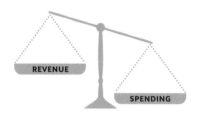

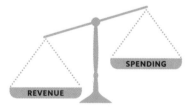

Deficit
A government runs a deficit when it spends more than it earns. The difference is made up by borrowing.

Surplus
A government that earns more than it spends can use the surplus to repay debts or stimulate the economy.

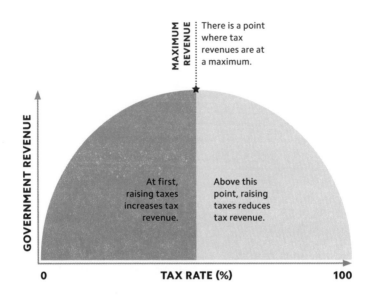

MAXIMUM REVENUE

There is a point where tax revenues are at a maximum.

GOVERNMENT REVENUE

At first, raising taxes increases tax revenue.

Above this point, raising taxes reduces tax revenue.

0   TAX RATE (%)   100

THE RIGHT AMOUNT OF TAX

It may seem common sense that raising tax rates increases the amount of money a government has to spend on public services. But in the 1980s, Arthur Laffer argued that high taxes discourage people from working and reduce output and so reduce tax revenue. Cutting taxes, he said, stimulates work and output and therefore boosts tax revenue. His simple graph, the Laffer Curve, shows the relationship between the tax rate and revenues. His argument was used to justify tax cuts in the 1980s but has since been challenged as too simplistic.

"If you tax people who work... you find a lot of people not working..."
Arthur Laffer

WHERE DOES TAX GO?

Public services are provided by the public sector (see p.41), although government agencies may also work with the private or voluntary sectors to deliver them. They are the services considered to be of benefit to society, though they vary by country and by political outlook. Mostly funded by tax, they are often free at the point of delivery. Some, like the fire brigade, are available to all. Many, such as schools, may depend on immigration status, and some exclude non-payers; for example, drivers must pay road tax.

HEALTH AND SOCIAL CARE

SOCIAL SECURITY

EDUCATION

UTILITIES

EMERGENCY SERVICES

LAW AND ORDER

TRANSPORT

DEFENCE

Expansionary policy aims to cut tax and raise public spending to increase demand and boost the economy.

Overspending may lead to inflation as prices are pushed up by unmet demand.

GOVERNMENT INTERVENTION

Governments try to steer their nation's economy in two ways: indirectly via the monetary policy of the central bank (see pp.58–59) and directly via their own fiscal policy. Fiscal policy aims to balance tax rates and public spending. In the 1930s, John Maynard Keynes argued that by influencing the amount of money flowing through the economy, the government can regulate business cycles (see pp.48–49), inflation (see pp.52–53), and unemployment (see p.64).

Removing money can reduce demand so much that recession is likely.

Contractionary policy aims to raise tax and cut public spending to reduce demand and control inflation.

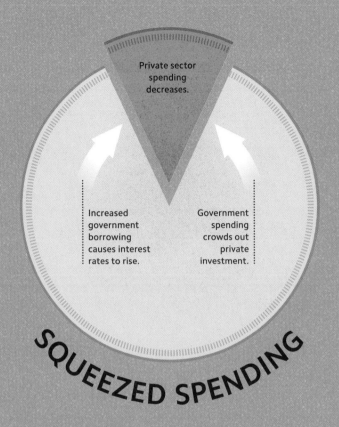

Private sector
spending
decreases.

Increased
government
borrowing
causes interest
rates to rise.

Government
spending
crowds out
private
investment.

SQUEEZED SPENDING

Government spending can result in "crowding out" – an
equivalent drop in private sector spending. If a government
increases spending on welfare, infrastructure, or industry, for
instance, private companies cannot compete in those sectors
as consumers may choose free or subsidized public services
over more costly private ones. More government borrowing
to fund spending may, in turn, cause interest rates to rise,
making it harder for private companies to borrow to fund
projects. But government spending does not always crowd
out private investment: in a declining economy, government
investment may generate jobs and income, which instead
stimulates private spending (see pp.46–47).

GOVERNMENT-FUELLED GROWTH

In the 1930s, John Maynard Keynes described the "Keynesian multiplier" – his theory that fiscal stimulus (investment by the government) helps the economy to flourish by boosting demand and therefore supply. His idea was that the original investment flows around the circular economy, multiplying with each iteration as demand continues to drive supply. Critics say the theory ignores the risk of the government crowding out private investment (see p.45) and the long-term effects of increased debt and higher taxes.

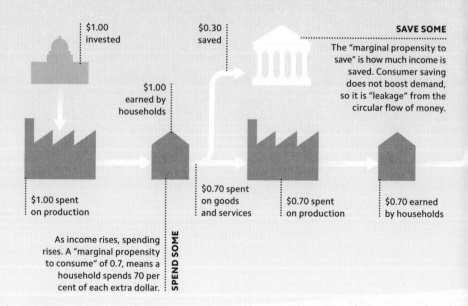

$1.00 invested

$0.30 saved

SAVE SOME

The "marginal propensity to save" is how much income is saved. Consumer saving does not boost demand, so it is "leakage" from the circular flow of money.

$1.00 earned by households

$1.00 spent on production

$0.70 spent on goods and services

$0.70 spent on production

$0.70 earned by households

As income rises, spending rises. A "marginal propensity to consume" of 0.7, means a household spends 70 per cent of each extra dollar.

SPEND SOME

> "The importance of money flows from it being a link between the present and the future."
> John Maynard Keynes

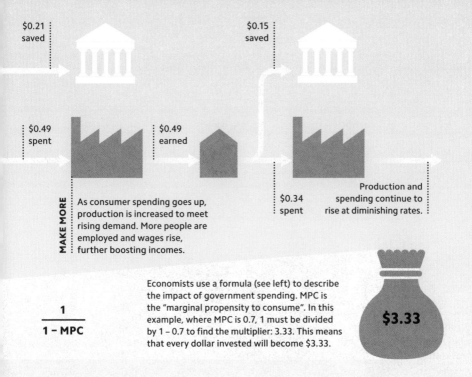

$0.21 saved

$0.49 spent

$0.49 earned

$0.15 saved

$0.34 spent

Production and spending continue to rise at diminishing rates.

MAKE MORE

As consumer spending goes up, production is increased to meet rising demand. More people are employed and wages rise, further boosting incomes.

$$\frac{1}{1-MPC}$$

Economists use a formula (see left) to describe the impact of government spending. MPC is the "marginal propensity to consume". In this example, where MPC is 0.7, 1 must be divided by 1 – 0.7 to find the multiplier: 3.33. This means that every dollar invested will become $3.33.

$3.33

Economies are rarely steady – they naturally fluctuate between periods of expansion and contraction. During a "boom", economic activity increases, consumers spend more, and unemployment falls. As this happens, market conditions become tighter: supply cannot keep up with the high demand, and businesses either need to spend more on workers or raise their prices or even both. Higher prices eventually put a brake on spending as people are restricted to what they can afford. The economy contracts and may enter a recession ("bust"). After a period of falling economic activity, prices fully adjust, demand hits a trough, and the cycle continues as the economy begins to grow once more.

Steady growth
Demand increases, prompting businesses to employ more people to boost output. Competition for workers causes wages to rise and consumer confidence booms.

Contraction
Consumers lose confidence and stop spending, and businesses lose confidence and slow investment – perhaps due to a stock market crash or rise in interest rates. As demand slides, output shrinks.

Rapid growth
Demand and output soar (boom). But if demand rises faster than output, prices may inflate and people may overinvest, making growth unsustainable. Eventually this results in a crash.

BOOM AND BUST

Economic bubble

A bubble forms when prices of things such as housing suddenly soar far above the real value. It pops when they crash back down.

Recession

Businesses reduce their output, using fewer resources, including labour. Unemployment rises and wages fall. As consumer spending and output go down, the economy slumps into a trough (bust).

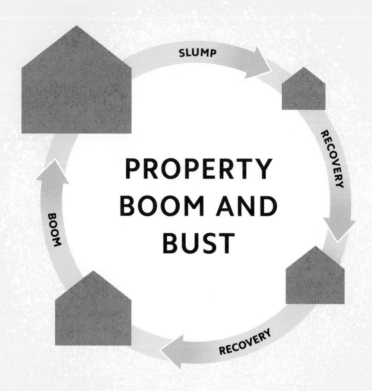

PROPERTY BOOM AND BUST

SLUMP

RECOVERY

BOOM

RECOVERY

The housing (or property) cycle is the pattern by which property prices rise, fall, and then recover, mirroring boom and bust in the wider economy (see pp.48–49). Prices boom as confidence grows and investors move into property. Prices then reach an unsustainable level, buyers disappear, and prices slump significantly. Finally, lower prices attract bargain hunters, and prices gradually recover. Only external intervention can moderate this cycle. For example, after the 2008 financial crisis, central banks carried out quantitative easing (see p.61), pumping money into their economies in a bid to cushion them from a housing cycle slump.

EXPECTATIONS GOVERN SPENDING

The permanent income hypothesis, introduced in 1957 by Milton Friedman, proposes that people's spending is spread evenly over time. When someone receives a boost in income, they will not immediately spend more. Instead, they base their spending on their "permanent income" – what they expect to be earning in the long-term. The hypothesis advises policymakers that a boost to income is only likely to trigger an increase in spending if the rise is perceived to be lasting.

Rising income
People spend more only if they expect their permanent income to rise. A one-off windfall is unlikely to trigger a sudden spending spree.

Falling income
People spend less if they expect their permanent income to fall. If someone doubts a windfall will last, they save more money for their future needs.

In all economies, prices vary over time. Inflation occurs when prices are rising but consumers' spending power does not keep up, so their money buys them less. It can be driven by rising demand (for example, if a country prints too much money) or by rising production costs. Typically, inflation is measured by the average price increase of a basket of selected goods in indices such as the Consumer Price Index (CPI; see p.55). Inflation means that a country's currency buys less, so the value of it diminishes. Gradual inflation is normal, but rapid inflation can lead to economic collapse.

RISING PRICES

Demand-pull inflation

This is when the availability of money and credit means that demand for goods and services rises much faster than a country's ability to increase production. The rising demand pulls prices upwards.

Hyperinflation

When the prices of goods and services rise by more than 50 per cent per month, this is hyperinflation. It can occur if a country prints too much money and so demand outstrips supply.

Cost-push inflation

This is when prices rise because of increased production costs, often caused by higherwages or raw material costs. There are no alternatives for consumers, so demand stays the same and prices rise.

> "[Inflation] is a way to take people's wealth from them without having to openly raise taxes."
> Thomas Sowell

UNEMPLOYMENT VS INFLATION

Developed in the 1950s by William Phillips, the Phillips curve suggests an inverse relationship between unemployment and inflation: as unemployment rises, wages – and prices – increase slowly; when unemployment falls, wages – and prices – rise rapidly. Rising wages and prices cause inflation (see pp.52–53). Phillips argued that, as unemployment falls, employers must raise wages to attract scarce labour. But periods of "stagflation" (economic stagnation along with high inflation) in the 1970s made economists adapt the model to take account of the role of people's expectations of future prices and wages (see p.51).

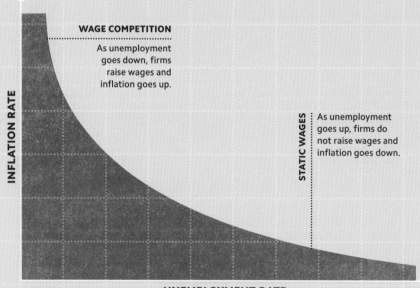

WAGE COMPETITION

As unemployment goes down, firms raise wages and inflation goes up.

STATIC WAGES

As unemployment goes up, firms do not raise wages and inflation goes down.

INFLATION RATE

UNEMPLOYMENT RATE

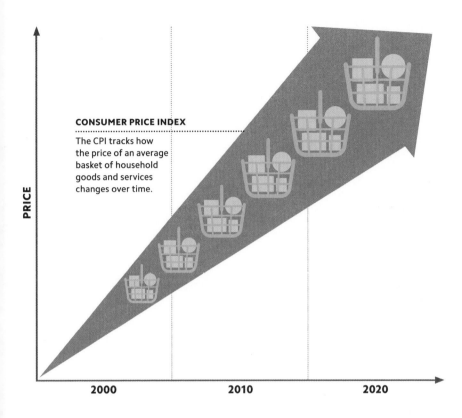

PRICE

2000   2010   2020

MEASURING INFLATION

A price index is a way to measure inflation by assessing how much a basket of selected goods and services changes in price over a period of time. Common indices across the world are the Consumer Price Index (CPI) for goods and services bought by households; the Wholesale Price Index (WPI) for the prices charged by wholesalers and manufacturers; and the Producer Price Index (PPI) for the prices received for output. Indices have a base of 100, so if a basket increases by 20 per cent, the new index will be 120.

PRICE VS SUPPLY

In the 16th century, after gold and silver were imported into the economy and minted into coins, prices went up. This led mathematician Nicolaus Copernicus to deduce that if the supply of money in an economy increases, prices will rise proportionally (assuming all other factors stay the same). Put simply, if more money becomes available, it is worth less. In 1911, Irving Fisher wrote an equation to explain the theory mathematically. This states that the total amount spent (M x V) will always be equal to the total amount received on those transactions (P x T).

$$M \times V = P \times T$$

Money supply
The quantity of money in an economy.

Velocity of circulation
How many times the money changes hands.

Average price level
The price at which items are sold.

Transactions
The number of times items are sold.

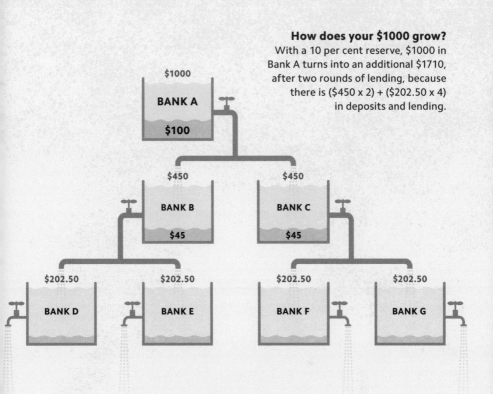

How does your $1000 grow?
With a 10 per cent reserve, $1000 in Bank A turns into an additional $1710, after two rounds of lending, because there is ($450 x 2) + ($202.50 x 4) in deposits and lending.

$1000

BANK A

$100

$450

BANK B

$45

$450

BANK C

$45

$202.50

BANK D

$202.50

BANK E

$202.50

BANK F

$202.50

BANK G

MAKING MONEY FROM MONEY

In a fractional reserve banking system, the central bank decides what proportion of deposits other banks must physically hold, in case of a rush to withdraw cash. If, say, this minimum reserve is 10 per cent, banks are free to lend the other 90 per cent of their deposits. When each loan is paid into another bank, it arrives as a deposit, meaning that the new bank can then lend out 90 per cent of its value – and so on. In this way, banks make money, increasing the supply available to borrowers.

> "Inflation is always and everywhere a monetary phenomenon."
> Milton Friedman

INFLATION TARGETING

Central banks may be required to keep inflation below a certain level (see p.60). They do this by raising base rates, which reduces spending in the economy. On the other hand, if there is not enough spending, the banks can lower base rates to boost credit.

INFLUENCING THE MONEY SUPPLY

Monetary policy refers to the set of actions used to control the supply of money in an economy. It is normally carried out by the central bank – as opposed to fiscal policy, which is set by the government (see p.44) – and most often involves setting a base interest rate that it charges commercial banks for borrowing money. This rate influences how much commercial banks charge consumers for their services, so it filters into the wider economy. If the base interest rate is higher, the money supply as a whole contracts, and borrowing and spending will be lower. An expansionary monetary policy would boost spending and borrowing with a lower base rate.

PRINTING MONEY

Central banks might try to boost economic activity by printing new money, so more is available for buying things. However, if there is an insufficient supply of products and services, too much money in circulation can cause rapid inflation.

QUANTITATIVE EASING

The central bank can buy or sell government debt (see p.61). Purchasing bonds issued by the government (also called sovereign debt) injects money into circulation and lowers interest rates on borrowing. By selling bonds from its account, the central bank can reduce how much money is in circulation.

CONTROLLING BANK LENDING

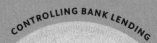

Central banks can free up or tighten lending by the nation's banks, and so increase or decrease the money supply, by lowering or raising the amount of money that banks must legally keep in reserve – cash they must physically keep in stock (see p.57).

LENDER OF LAST RESORT

The central bank supports commercial banks that get into trouble due to customers defaulting on loans or due to a run on cash (when too many people withdraw their savings all at once).

CENTRAL BANK

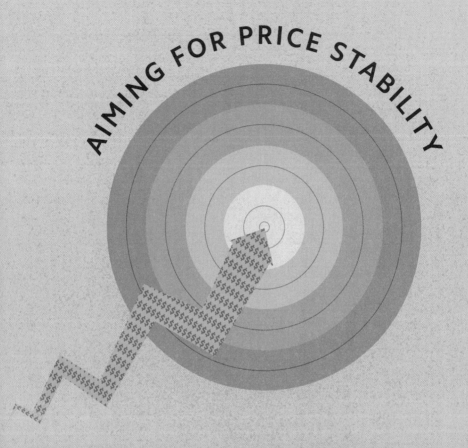

AIMING FOR PRICE STABILITY

Inflation targeting is when central banks use monetary
policy (see pp.58–59) to attempt to keep inflation within a
desired range, often around 2 per cent. They usually do this
by adjusting interest rates. The intention is to avoid the
destabilizing effects of high inflation. From the 1990s,
economists believed that maintaining price stability was key
to economic growth. However, following the 2008 recession,
some have argued that inflation targeting gets in the way
of more crucial goals, such as targeting exchange rates,
unemployment, or overall national income.

"... sufficient injections of money will ultimately always reverse a deflation."
Ben Bernanke

ECONOMIC GROWTH

Quantitative easing

A central bank can control the amount of money circulating using quantitative easing (QE). The bank buys government bonds, pushing their price up. This, in turn, pushes interest rates down (see pp.144–145), making it easier for people to borrow and spend.

Helicopter money

A more extreme alternative to QE, helicopter money is when large amounts of money are distributed directly to the public (e.g. in the form of relief payments) – like a helicopter drop of supplies in an emergency.

Negative interest rates

By charging interest on money deposits in commercial banks (a negative interest rate), a central bank can encourage the banks to spend and lend their cash reserves rather than losing money by holding on to them.

DRASTIC ACTION

During an economic crisis, such as the 2008 recession, traditional monetary policy methods (see pp.58–59) involving tightening or loosening the money supply may fail. In these abnormal situations, when drastic action is required, central banks may resort to other, "unconventional" methods to jump-start the economy, including quantitative easing, helicopter money, and negative interest rates.

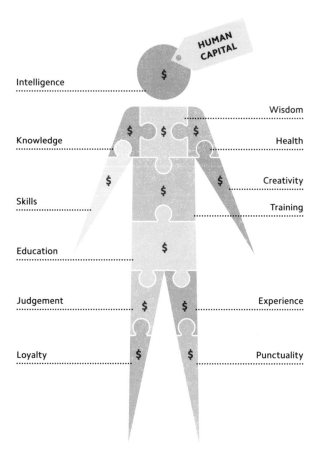

Intelligence

Wisdom

Knowledge

Health

Creativity

Skills

Training

Education

Judgement

Experience

Loyalty

Punctuality

A PERSON'S WORTH

Human capital is the economic value of the knowledge, skills, and experience of a worker. Companies can increase their human capital by investing in training their workforce; countries can do so by improving educational opportunities. Investments are made in the hope of future economic benefit, through improved productivity or better employee retention. Higher human capital may lead to higher profits for firms and growth for countries, but this value can depreciate – for instance, if skilled workers move elsewhere.

WAGES ADJUST SLOWLY

When demand for goods and labour rises, wages normally rise as a result. When demand falls, it could be expected that wages would also fall, but they tend to "stick" – stay the same. Reducing wages is unpopular and is resisted by workers and unions. Therefore, rather than pay individuals less, employers are more likely to lay off staff during a recession, causing a larger rise in unemployment than would otherwise be necessary. Sticky wages explain, in part, why unemployment can persist and why wages do not just fall to eliminate it.

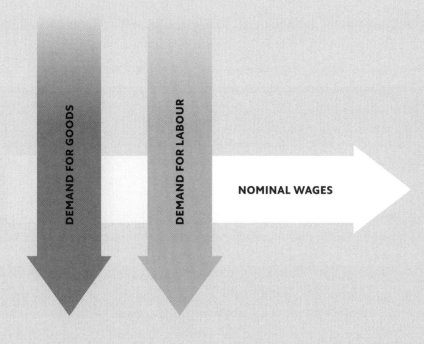

DEMAND FOR GOODS

DEMAND FOR LABOUR

NOMINAL WAGES

CAN WORK/
CAN'T WORK

Unemployment occurs when people who are willing and able to work cannot find a job. The unemployment rate is the number of people unemployed divided by the total workforce. It reflects the health of an economy: a higher rate results in lower economic output. The three main types of unemployment are: cyclical, when staff are laid off as demand decreases during a recession; structural, caused by inefficiencies, such as lack of skills; and frictional, when workers are between jobs. All economies have a baseline level of unemployment, below which it is hard to go because without frictional unemployment it is difficult for employers to fill vacancies efficiently.

A FLEXIBLE WORKFORCE

A gig economy is a labour market with a high level of short-term contracts and freelance work, in which workers are not paid a fixed salary but only for the jobs they carry out. Couriers, cab services, and catering all have a high number of gig workers. The gig economy offers companies flexibility, enabling them to adjust their workforce more easily and cheaply. Workers also gain flexibility, choosing when and where to work. On the other hand, gig workers may sacrifice traditional employee benefits such as pensions, as well as job security.

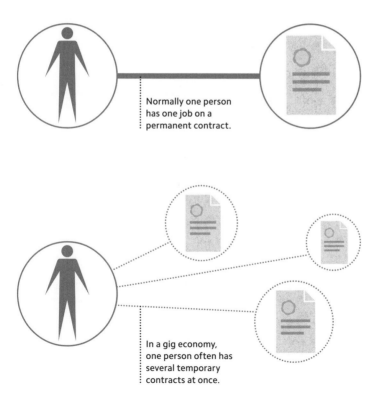

Normally one person has one job on a permanent contract.

In a gig economy, one person often has several temporary contracts at once.

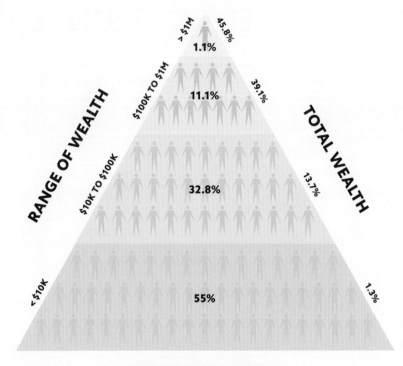

RANGE OF WEALTH

TOTAL WEALTH

> $1M — 1.1% — 45.8%

$100K TO $1M — 11.1% — 39.1%

$10K TO $100K — 32.8% — 13.7%

< $10K — 55% — 1.3%

NUMBER OF ADULTS

LIFE ISN'T FAIR

Economic inequality is the unequal distribution of resources. There are two types: income and wealth inequality. Income inequality may occur if a person works in a low-paying sector, or is part of a group (e.g. women) that is discriminated against. Wealth inequality arises when assets, such as property, are owned by some but not others. Governments can try to combat inequality with taxes or investment targeted at poorer groups, whose economic prospects may be limited by lack of access to services such as education.

MEASURING INEQUALITY

The Gini index is a way of assessing inequality by measuring how equally income is distributed in a country. If a country has a Gini coefficient of zero, everybody is earning exactly the same amount, while if it has a score of one, all income is earned by a single person. The average Gini coefficient has risen steadily over the past few centuries, indicating a rise in global inequality. Although the highest Gini coefficients tend to be found in low-income countries, some rich nations, notably the US, have high income inequality.

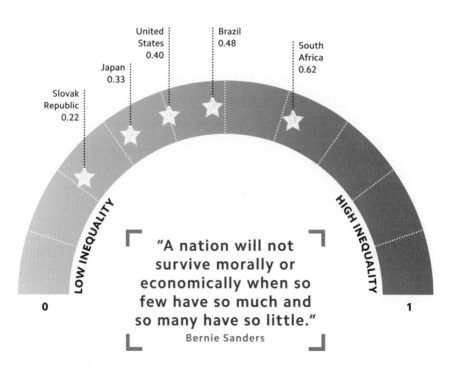

Slovak Republic 0.22

Japan 0.33

United States 0.40

Brazil 0.48

South Africa 0.62

LOW INEQUALITY

HIGH INEQUALITY

0

1

"A nation will not survive morally or economically when so few have so much and so many have so little."
Bernie Sanders

CHOICE
CONSEQ

S AND
UENCES

Economics starts by looking at choice because the decisions about what to produce and what to consume drive all economic exchanges. Choice requires the selection of one option over alternatives, and the consequences of many individual choices can be vast. Although economists would say that markets mostly do a good job of matching up people's choices about what they want to consume with what is produced, sometimes markets do not deliver ideal outcomes. Economists analyse these market failures and the reasons behind them – for example, when people have limited access to information or when the desired social outcome varies from the market choice.

CARROTS AND STICKS

Most economic theories assume that, when making choices, people usually look to improve their economic circumstances. In other words, people respond to financial incentives and disincentives – carrots and sticks. These can therefore be a tool for changing economic behaviour. A pay rise might spur people to work harder, while producers may boost supply if they can sell their product for a higher price. A tax rise on an item, such as alcohol or plastic bags, can discourage use. A subsidy, on the other hand, might be used to encourage people to insulate their homes.

MONEY

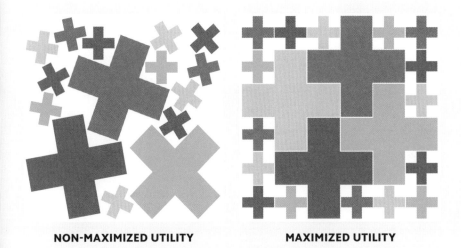

NON-MAXIMIZED UTILITY   MAXIMIZED UTILITY

GETTING MORE
FOR YOUR MONEY

Economists model consumer choice by assuming
that people want to get the most utility (value or
satisfaction) from the goods and services available
to them. Nobody can have everything: all consumers
face constraint – for example, on their money or time.
Therefore, they choose the best combination of goods
and services that maximizes their utility. When prices
change and a consumer's situation does not, they
re-optimize, selecting a new solution. By assuming
this "utility maximization", economists are able
to build more complex market models.

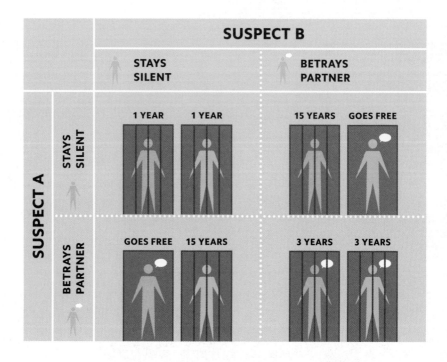

SELF-INTEREST VS GROUP INTEREST

The "prisoner's dilemma" is a model in game theory in which the best possible outcome for each individual is not the best collective outcome. Two suspects are each offered a deal: confess and implicate your partner and you can walk free – if your partner stays silent. But if you stay silent and your partner talks, you will get a very long sentence. The best collective outcome is for both suspects to stay silent, but by doing this, they each risk maximum harm. This means they are both better off talking. That way, they get the worst collective outcome, but not the worst for each individual.

MUTUAL SELF-INTEREST

The "stag hunt" is a model in game theory in which cooperation leads to the best collective result. Two hunters go looking for food. If they act alone, they could each catch a rabbit. But if they work together, they may get the far greater prize of a stag to share, but they sacrifice the chance of a rabbit. The hunters should cooperate because the best outcome for each individual is also the best collective outcome. However, each hunter is dependent on the other and risks walking away with nothing. How each chooses to act will depend on what they trust the other will do.

		HUNTER B	
		HUNTS FOR STAG	HUNTS FOR RABBIT
HUNTER A	HUNTS FOR STAG	HALF A STAG EACH	NO STAG — RABBIT
	HUNTS FOR RABBIT	RABBIT — NO STAG	RABBIT — RABBIT

OVERUSE

The "tragedy of the commons" is a term for the tendency of a resource that no-one owns to be overused. For example, on common land where there are no restrictions or costs, each farmer has an incentive to graze as many sheep as they can. If too many farmers do that, then the land will become depleted for everyone. Instead, the farmers should cooperate and use the land in a sustainable way. Studying the Maasai in Africa, Elinor Ostrom found that they used "polycentric governance" – a system where the use of the resource was agreed on, and the tragedy avoided.

LOW DEMAND

A few sheep can graze sustainably without causing harm. One extra sheep has little impact.

HIGH DEMAND

When too many sheep graze the land, it becomes depleted. No sheep feed well.

SUPPLY DRIES UP

There comes a point where too many sheep use the land and grazing is destroyed for everyone.

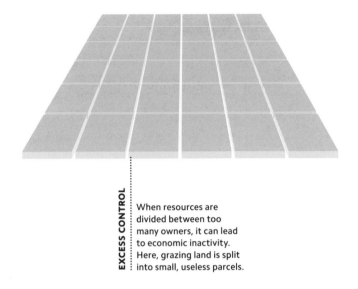

When resources are divided between too many owners, it can lead to economic inactivity. Here, grazing land is split into small, useless parcels.

UNDERUSE

When multiple owners control a resource and each party has the right to exclude the others from using it but cannot make use of it independently, a breakdown of coordination can occur. This is the "tragedy of the anticommons" and it can lead to underutilization. Attempts to use such a resource (often land or intellectual property) can be delayed or not happen at all. For example, a public infrastructure development could be held up if many landholders have to be bought out, or a television programme might be released without its original soundtrack because too many rights deals have to be struck.

SELLER'S
KNOWLEDGE

EFFICIENT
PRICE

BUYER'S
KNOWLEDGE

UNEQUAL KNOWLEDGE

Asymmetric information is where one party knows more than the other when making a deal. Such situations are not perfectly competitive and can result in prices that do not reflect the true value of a product or service. Either sellers or buyers can have the advantage. For example, someone selling their house knows more about it that a potential buyer, but an antiques expert browsing a car-boot sale may know more about an item than the seller. In markets characterized by asymmetry, parties try to minimize the problem – for example, by offering guarantees.

SELLER'S KNOWLEDGE

HIGH
PRICE

BUYER'S
KNOWLEDGE

SELLER'S
KNOWLEDGE

BUYER'S KNOWLEDGE

LOW
PRICE

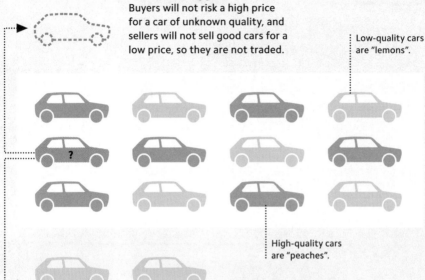

Peaches disappear
Buyers will not risk a high price for a car of unknown quality, and sellers will not sell good cars for a low price, so they are not traded.

Low-quality cars are "lemons".

High-quality cars are "peaches".

Only lemons remain
Some buyers will risk a low price for an unknown car and sellers will accept it for a low-quality car so lemons are traded.

THE COST OF UNEQUAL KNOWLEDGE

In a "lemon market", information asymmetry (see opposite) is so severe that a market fails entirely. The term was coined in 1970 by George Akerlof in a study of used cars. In this market, the sellers know more than buyers about the condition of the cars. If they cannot prove a car is high quality, a buyer will not pay what it should be worth, and the market for the best cars dries up, leaving only low-priced, low-quality cars. To prevent this, sellers might offer guarantees or warranties or establish a trusted brand.

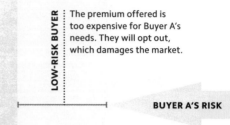

The premium offered is too expensive for Buyer A's needs. They will opt out, which damages the market.

BUYER A'S RISK

INSURER'S INTENDED RISK

BUYER B'S RISK

BUYER C'S RISK

Buyer C's high level of risk will cost the insurer money. If the cost of premiums rises, Buyer B will be priced out of the market as with Buyer A.

HIGH-RISK BUYER

RISK VS INFORMATION

Adverse selection is a situation that can arise as a result of information asymmetry (see p.76). It occurs when one party in a deal exploits the fact that they know more than the other. Adverse selection has particular implications for the insurance market. If a seller has little to go on when assessing the risk of a potential buyer, they may assume that the buyer is high risk purely because they want insurance. As a result, they may charge an unduly high price. To prevent adverse selection, the seller can screen the buyer to more accurately assess their level of risk.

The terms of the agreement have a balance of risk and reward for both parties.

SELLER'S RISK

BUYER'S RISK

The terms of the agreement have a balance of risk and reward for both parties.

INFORMATION VS RISK

Moral hazard can arise due to asymmetrical information (see p.76). It occurs when one party to an agreement is exposed to greater risk because the other party changes their behaviour after the deal is agreed. For example, a buyer of home insurance may take fewer precautions to keep their home secure because the seller now bears the risk for them. Moral hazard contrasts with adverse selection (see opposite) because the asymmetry occurs after the agreement, rather than at the time.

SELLER'S RISK

BUYER'S RISK

The seller's risk is increased if the buyer changes their behaviour after the agreement is made.

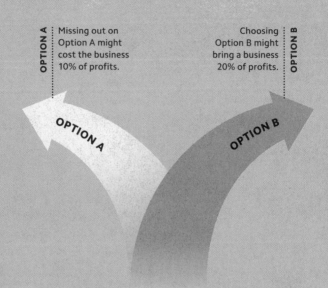

| RETURN ON BEST OPTION NOT CHOSEN (OPTION A) | – | RETURN ON OPTION CHOSEN (OPTION B) | = | OPPORTUNITY COST |

OPTION A
Missing out on Option A might cost the business 10% of profits.

OPTION B
Choosing Option B might bring a business 20% of profits.

OPTION A

OPTION B

THE ROAD NOT TAKEN

The economic idea of "opportunity cost" arises because resources – including people's time – are limited. It describes how the cost of any course of action (whether someone pays money for it or not) includes all the things that are therefore not done. If a person takes up a free ticket to see a movie rather than work, then the cost of their trip includes the work they have not done. Opportunity cost should therefore be factored into cost-benefit analysis – a decision-making process that weighs the costs of a choice against its benefits.

WHY SAVING IS BAD

Reducing spending to save money is generally considered prudent, and it may seem particularly sensible during a recession – when the national economy is shrinking. However, the more households do this, the more it can fuel the recession. If consumers cut back, demand for goods and services falls and suppliers' income also falls. They then have less money to invest in production, including employing people. The result is lower demand and an economic situation that is worse for everybody.

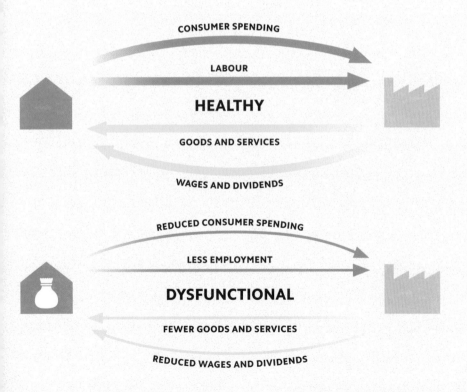

CONSUMER SPENDING

LABOUR

HEALTHY

GOODS AND SERVICES

WAGES AND DIVIDENDS

REDUCED CONSUMER SPENDING

LESS EMPLOYMENT

DYSFUNCTIONAL

FEWER GOODS AND SERVICES

REDUCED WAGES AND DIVIDENDS

INCOME DRIVES BEHAVIOUR

The income effect and the substitution effect are ways of understanding how consumer behaviour alters in response to changes in the market. The income effect focuses on consumption caused by changes in price. If prices go down and a consumer's income remains the same, then their purchasing power increases, meaning they can buy more units. Therefore, demand goes up. Equally, if prices rise, then demand falls. The substitution effect explains how, if the price of a product rises when income does not, then consumers may find a cheaper alternative instead. Similarly, even a modest reduction in the price of a more expensive brand may persuade consumers to give it a try.

As purchasing power rises, consumers spend more.

INCOME EFFECT

As purchasing power falls, consumers spend less.

The income effect
This considers how variations in purchasing power influence consumers' spending patterns.

> **"The price of every thing rises and falls... and with every such change the purchasing power of money changes."**
> Alfred Marshall

SUBSTITUTION EFFECT

As prices drop, consumers may not just buy more, but might switch to more expensive items.

As prices rise, consumers may not just buy less, but might switch to cheaper items.

The substitution effect
This looks at how changes in price can encourage consumers to switch to alternative products and brands.

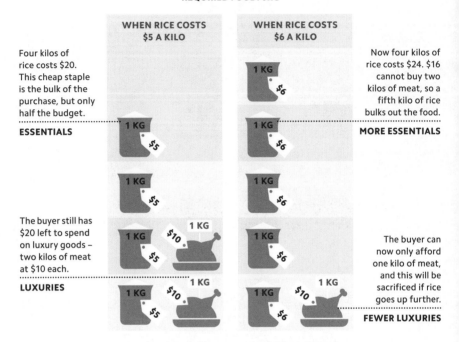

SHOPPING LIST
BUDGET: $40
REQUIRED FOOD: 6KG

WHEN RICE COSTS $5 A KILO

Four kilos of rice costs $20. This cheap staple is the bulk of the purchase, but only half the budget.

ESSENTIALS

The buyer still has $20 left to spend on luxury goods – two kilos of meat at $10 each.

LUXURIES

WHEN RICE COSTS $6 A KILO

Now four kilos of rice costs $24. $16 cannot buy two kilos of meat, so a fifth kilo of rice bulks out the food.

MORE ESSENTIALS

The buyer can now only afford one kilo of meat, and this will be sacrificed if rice goes up further.

FEWER LUXURIES

RISING PRICES CAN BOOST DEMAND

When the price of a product goes up, demand usually falls because people buy less or switch to a cheaper alternative. However, the opposite is true with Giffen goods – as their price increases, so can demand. Giffen goods are typically inexpensive essential items with few substitutes. If they rise in price, a consumer has less to spend on non-essentials. In order to meet their basic needs, they may buy more of the Giffen good. Even though it has risen in price, it is still the cheapest option.

Positive side-effects
Building a new factory
will provide jobs for the
community and support
other local businesses.

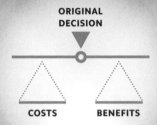

ORIGINAL
DECISION

COSTS   BENEFITS

Negative side-effects
The new factory may outcompete
existing employers, causing
them to close. It may
also produce pollution.

DECISIONS HAVE CONSEQUENCES

An externality occurs when production or consumption results
in costs or benefits for an unrelated third party. Individuals,
organizations, or society as a whole can be affected. Externalities
can be positive, such as the advancement of public knowledge
from research and development. Negative externalities include
pollution. The impact of these can be lessened by compensating
those affected, by taxing or regulating those responsible,
and ultimately by prohibiting the activity altogether.

THE POLLUTER MUST PAY

The cost of environmental damage, such as pollution, is often borne by society – not the producer responsible. If there is such a negative externality (see p.85), the price of a good does not account for the social cost of producing it, which means the market mechanism fails. To correct this, the state can intervene with "Pigovian" taxes to make the polluter pay. These were proposed by Arthur Pigou in the 1920s to redistribute the externality cost to the producer and, ultimately, to the market, thereby reflecting a truer cost to consumers.

ENVIRONMENTAL TAXES

STATE

POLLUTING FACTORY

CLEAN FACTORY

ENVIRONMENTAL SUBSIDIES

State intervention
To protect the environment, the state may discourage polluters with high taxes and give subsidies to those who clean up their act.

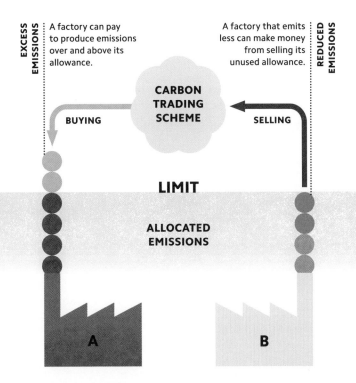

A factory can pay to produce emissions over and above its allowance.

A factory that emits less can make money from selling its unused allowance.

CARBON TRADING SCHEME

BUYING

SELLING

LIMIT

ALLOCATED EMISSIONS

A

B

TRADING EMISSIONS

Many industrial processes emit greenhouse gases, such as carbon dioxide, which contribute to global warming. Emission trading schemes aim to address this problem by using financial incentives to change behaviour. They put the burden of reducing emissions onto those responsible so those who pollute the most, pay the most. Under these schemes, governments set a maximum level of emissions from each producer. If a factory emits more, then they must buy credits for each extra unit of pollution. A factory that emits less than its allowance can sell its unused credits. Permitted levels are normally lowered gradually over time.

THERO
MARKE

E O F

T S

Markets are physical or virtual places where buyers and sellers make exchanges. The parties to these transactions make an agreement based on demand (how much of the item is wanted) and supply (how much is available). Guided by rising or falling prices, demand and supply will converge at an optimum level, or equilibrium, where the quantity demanded matches the quantity supplied. However, not all markets are alike, and outcomes depend on many factors, including the organization of the market, the number of competing firms, and the technology involved. Nor are markets perfect; they can fail. Economists try to understand what might cause failure and what can be done about it.

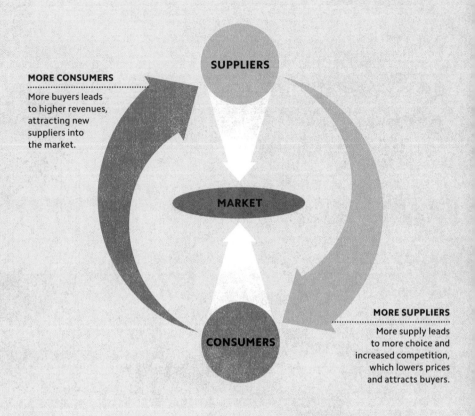

SUPPLIERS

MORE CONSUMERS
More buyers leads
to higher revenues,
attracting new
suppliers into
the market.

MARKET

MORE SUPPLIERS
More supply leads
to more choice and
increased competition,
which lowers prices
and attracts buyers.

CONSUMERS

MUTUAL BENEFITS

A two-sided platform market is a privately owned marketplace
that connects suppliers and consumers, usually charging a
commission on sales. Examples include mobile phone app stores,
online ride-hailing services, and holiday rental sites. This type of
market increases its value to sellers by adding more buyers, and
vice versa. Connecting more of each group means it can benefit
from indirect network effects (see p.115), increasing the value of
the platform. To achieve growth, platforms often subsidize one
group, so buyers may pay zero commission, or less than sellers.

EFFICIENT ISN'T ALWAYS FAIR

Pareto efficiency is a way of assessing whether the distribution of resources is efficient or not. The idea was first introduced in 1906 by Vilfredo Pareto. A distribution between two or more parties is Pareto efficient when it is not possible to make one party better off without making another worse off. Efficiency does not require the allocation to be equal or fair. If a distribution of resources is not Pareto efficient, then it means there is an unexploited opportunity hidden somewhere – for example, in the case of a deadweight loss (see p.97).

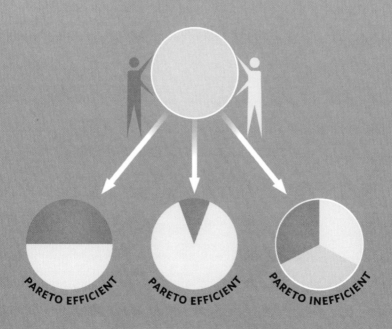

PARETO EFFICIENT

PARETO EFFICIENT

PARETO INEFFICIENT

IN IT TO WIN IT

Competition is the process by which firms attempt to gain sales and increase profits. Economists distinguish different types – from perfect competition through to monopolies (see p.96). Factors that determine which type of competition exists include costs of entry to the market, the degree of differentiation between products, economies of scale (see pp.32–33), the amount of information available, and the behaviour of firms in the market. Firms make no profit in a perfectly competitive market, but are able to profit in other "imperfect" forms.

"In economic life competition is never completely lacking, but hardly ever is it perfect."
Joseph Schumpeter

Perfect competition
This is the most competitive market possible. Entry is easy so there are many suppliers, consumers can easily find alternatives, and everyone has the same information. Prices are dictated by supply and demand, so are near or at production cost.

Monopolistic competition
There are fewer suppliers in this kind of market so they can set prices above production costs, within limits. This is because consumers can still find alternatives if prices are too high, so firms must differentiate their products to make a profit.

Oligopoly
This type of market is dominated by few suppliers because of the costs involved in entry. Firms can choose what to produce, but their market power creates a risk that they will work together to coordinate their prices at a high level.

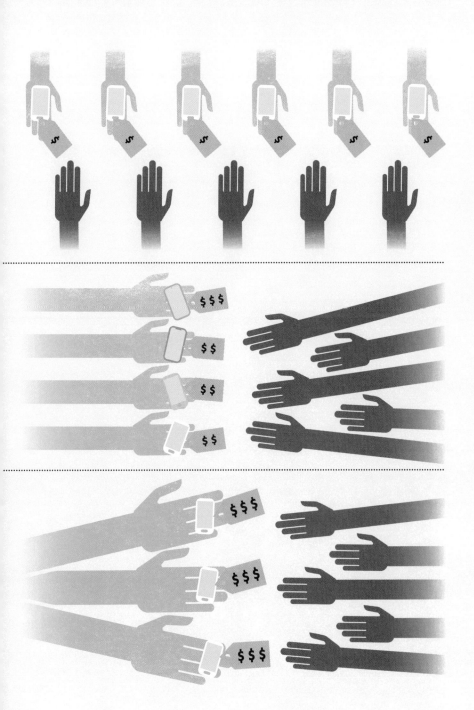

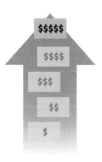

Ascending auction
In an English auction, buyers drop out as the bidding goes up until finally only one bidder is left.

Descending auction
In a Dutch auction, the auctioner starts with a high price, then drops it until a bidder shouts "Mine!"

First-price sealed bid
Each bidder places a single bid in a sealed envelope. The envelopes are then opened and the highest bid wins.

Second-price sealed bid
As with first-price sealed bids, the highest bidder wins, but here they pay the price of the second highest bid.

BIDDING TO BUY

In economics, auction theory is a general mechanism in which parties bid for a good or service. The price is not set in advance, but auctioneers design the sale to maximize the price paid by competing bidders, who keep their limits secret. If the true value of an item is not known there is an incentive to bid too high (the "winner's curse") – and second-price auctions are designed to correct this.

COLLUSION AND CONTROL

A cartel is a group of independent organizations who collectively set the prices of their products or control their supply. This collusion changes the market for their goods from a competitive one to a monopoly (see p.96). In such markets, buyers tend to face higher prices, lower quality, and reduced choice. As such, cartels are generally illegal, and the businesses involved risk prosecution by the competition authorities (see p.98). Companies that inform on their partners in crime can receive lower fines.

DOMINATING THE MARKET

Traditionally, a "monopoly" is defined as a single firm that supplies to the whole market; in law, it means one firm is dominant. A monopoly firm has the power to maximize profits by producing less (to keep demand high) and charging more than a competitive market (see pp.92–93). This is inefficient as it reduces the total possible benefit to an economy (see opposite). Monopolies may be supported by legal or structural barriers that exclude or undermine rivals. Their impact is mostly negative, especially on consumers, but they can have positive effects, too.

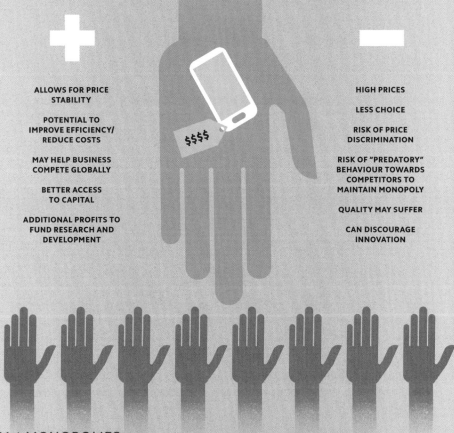

+

ALLOWS FOR PRICE STABILITY

POTENTIAL TO IMPROVE EFFICIENCY/ REDUCE COSTS

MAY HELP BUSINESS COMPETE GLOBALLY

BETTER ACCESS TO CAPITAL

ADDITIONAL PROFITS TO FUND RESEARCH AND DEVELOPMENT

—

HIGH PRICES

LESS CHOICE

RISK OF PRICE DISCRIMINATION

RISK OF "PREDATORY" BEHAVIOUR TOWARDS COMPETITORS TO MAINTAIN MONOPOLY

QUALITY MAY SUFFER

CAN DISCOURAGE INNOVATION

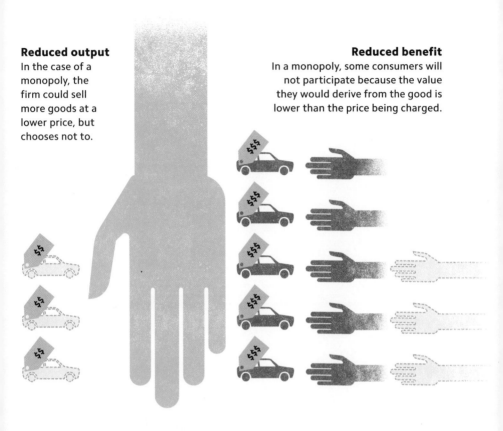

Reduced output
In the case of a monopoly, the firm could sell more goods at a lower price, but chooses not to.

Reduced benefit
In a monopoly, some consumers will not participate because the value they would derive from the good is lower than the price being charged.

THE COST OF NOT COMPETING

A deadweight loss is the reduction in total economic benefit that arises when supply and demand (see p.25) are not in equilibrium, so products and services become over- or underpriced. It measures the value of deals that do not happen due to, for example, monopolies (see opposite), taxes, subsidies, minimum wages, and maximum pricing like rent control. Overpriced and underpriced goods and services can lead to fewer items being sold, so both suppliers and consumers miss out.

DETERRING UNFAIR BEHAVIOUR

Antitrust is the mix of laws and regulatory practices that aim to ensure markets are competitive. It addresses three main areas. Firstly, it makes it an offence to form a cartel (see p.95), where businesses work together to raise or fix prices. Secondly, it imposes a set of rules on monopolies (see p.96) to stop them exploiting their position to the detriment of consumers. Finally, it may prevent mergers and acquisitions between businesses that will make markets less competitive. Antitrust rules are often backed up with legal requirements to behave better and by punishments like fines or, ultimately, the offending company being broken up.

Cartel agreements
The members of a cartel do not compete with one another, but instead join forces to control prices or supply. Antitrust laws are required to tackle:

PRICE FIXING

DIVIDING UP MARKETS

RIGGING BIDS

AGREEING TO CUT OUTPUT

> "Antitrust law [is] about protecting competition itself on behalf of the public."
> Al Franken

Single firm conduct

Competition may also be hampered if one company dominates, or monopolizes, a market. Antitrust laws target monopolies in order to prevent:

UNFAIR PRICING

PRICING TO EXCLUDE COMPETITORS

LIMITING PRODUCTION

EXCLUSIVE CONTRACTS

Mergers and acquisitions

Mergers and acquisitions may have a negative impact on market dynamics, reducing competition. Antitrust measures aim to control these effects:

HIGHER PRICES FOR RIVALS

PRICING TO WEAKEN TARGET

ELIMINATING DISRUPTERS/ MAVERICKS

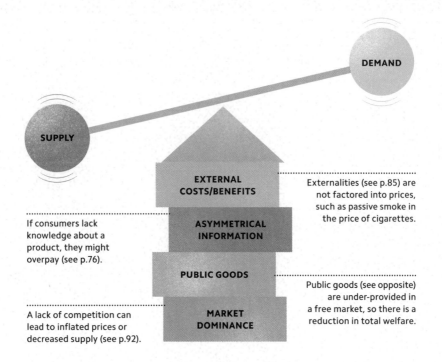

DEMAND

SUPPLY

EXTERNAL COSTS/BENEFITS

Externalities (see p.85) are not factored into prices, such as passive smoke in the price of cigarettes.

ASYMMETRICAL INFORMATION

If consumers lack knowledge about a product, they might overpay (see p.76).

PUBLIC GOODS

Public goods (see opposite) are under-provided in a free market, so there is a reduction in total welfare.

MARKET DOMINANCE

A lack of competition can lead to inflated prices or decreased supply (see p.92).

FREE MARKETS MAKE MISTAKES

Classic economic theory states that free markets will run efficiently, with supply equalling demand and all resources being allocated in a way that maximizes benefit and minimizes waste (see p.24). However, sometimes markets fail. When prices do not reflect the full cost or the full benefit of goods and services, supply and demand can become out of balance, leading to the inefficient distribution of resources. Governments often step in to solve market failures by introducing legislation or subsidies, and providing public goods.

FREE MARKETS DON'T LIKE FREEBIES

A good is public when it costs no more to provide it to, say, 100 people than to one, and it is not possible to exclude nonpayers from using it. In economic theory, these features mean public goods like parks and police forces may not be supplied in a free market because they are not profitable for private companies. Instead, they tend to be delivered by governments. Club goods are similar, in that many people can enjoy them at the same time. But nonpayers can be stopped from using them, often via legal or technological means.

EXCLUDABLE · **NONEXCLUDABLE**

Private goods
This type of good is rival (one person's use diminishes it or limits another's use) and excludable (nonpayers can be prevented from consuming it).

Common goods
These are rival but nonexcludable. For example, catching fish reduces available stocks, but it can be difficult to stop nonpayers fishing.

RIVAL

NONRIVAL

Club goods
These are nonrival but excludable, so user numbers can be limited. Examples include sport events and subscription-based streaming.

Public goods
These goods are both nonrival and nonexcludable – for example, many people can benefit from street lights without paying.

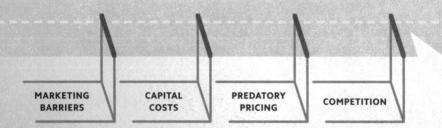

MARKETING BARRIERS

CAPITAL COSTS

PREDATORY PRICING

COMPETITION

MARKET

THOU SHALT NOT PASS

Barriers to entry are the factors that make it difficult for firms to enter new markets or for workers to gain employment in certain sectors. Barriers to entry may occur naturally, because of high start-up costs, or they can be imposed by government – for example, through difficult registration requirements or licensing fees. Existing companies can also exert pressure on startups, by buying them out or by lobbying the government to create further obstacles. Barriers to entry sometimes occur when one company dominates a market so strongly that it is virtually impossible for others to compete.

A SINGLE SOLUTION

Natural monopolies can arise in markets where fixed start-up
costs are so high that a venture is only economically viable
if one supplier serves the entire market. A single supplier
can achieve the economies of scale needed to offset the initial
expense and reduce costs enough to sell at prices consumers
can afford. Two competing firms would face the same start-up
costs but neither could attract as many customers, so prices
would be higher and fewer units would be sold. This is often
seen in markets such as utilities and public transport.

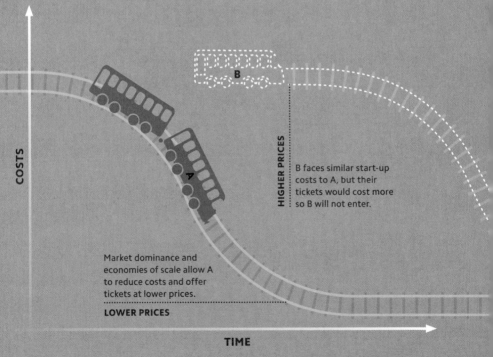

COSTS

HIGHER PRICES

B faces similar start-up
costs to A, but their
tickets would cost more
so B will not enter.

Market dominance and
economies of scale allow A
to reduce costs and offer
tickets at lower prices.

LOWER PRICES

TIME

MAXIMIZING GAINS

Welfare economics is about the gains achieved by the parties in a transaction. If a consumer buys an item for less than they were willing to pay for it, this gain is the "consumer surplus". If the item sells for more than it cost the seller, this is the "producer surplus". Together, these make up the "community surplus" – the total benefit achieved by both parties. When supply and demand (see p.25) are balanced in a free market, prices will set themselves at a point that maximizes the community surplus. But if conditions change (for example, due to subsidies, taxes, or monopolies), this can create a deadweight loss (see p.97) and result in an overall community loss.

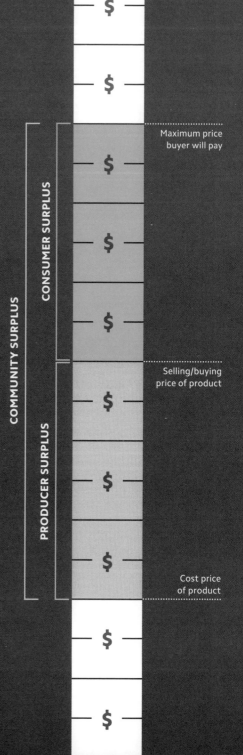

Maximum price buyer will pay

CONSUMER SURPLUS

COMMUNITY SURPLUS

Selling/buying price of product

PRODUCER SURPLUS

Cost price of product

THE COST OF THE DEAL

As well as having production costs, every trade incurs transaction costs – the cost of finding the customer and facilitating the exchange. For example, when selling a property, transaction costs include advertising, legal fees, and the estate agent's commission. Businesses analyse their transaction costs to see whether it is more efficient to do the operations in-house or outsource them to other suppliers. Transaction costs affect returns on investment, so they are an important figure for investors to consider.

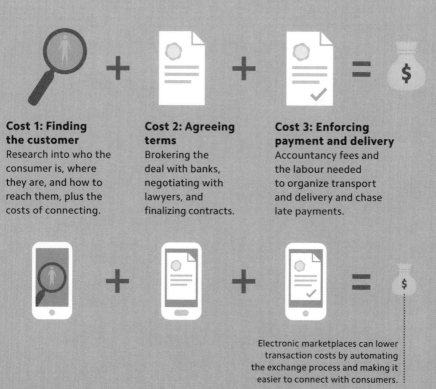

Cost 1: Finding the customer
Research into who the consumer is, where they are, and how to reach them, plus the costs of connecting.

Cost 2: Agreeing terms
Brokering the deal with banks, negotiating with lawyers, and finalizing contracts.

Cost 3: Enforcing payment and delivery
Accountancy fees and the labour needed to organize transport and delivery and chase late payments.

Electronic marketplaces can lower transaction costs by automating the exchange process and making it easier to connect with consumers.

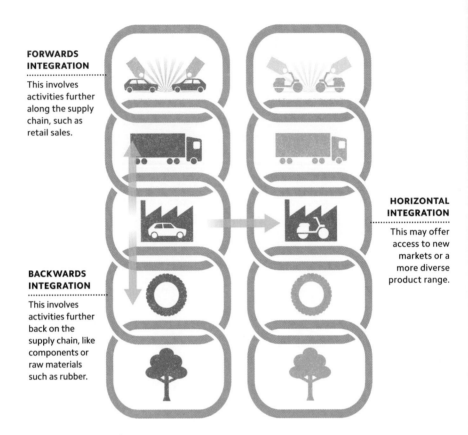

FORWARDS INTEGRATION

This involves activities further along the supply chain, such as retail sales.

HORIZONTAL INTEGRATION

This may offer access to new markets or a more diverse product range.

BACKWARDS INTEGRATION

This involves activities further back on the supply chain, like components or raw materials such as rubber.

GROWTH BY ACQUISITION

Vertical and horizontal integration are two different business growth strategies. Vertical growth means integrating more of the supply chain into a business. For example, a car manufacturer could buy a tyre factory to improve supply efficiency and reduce costs, and a dealership to get direct access to consumers. Horizontal growth is when one business buys another at a similar level on the supply chain. So, the car manufacturer might acquire a rival manufacturer to reduce competition or increase market share.

MONEY FOR NOTHING

Rent seeking is when a person or organization tries to increase their share of existing wealth, rather than creating more themselves. Whatever amount (rent) they gain, another party loses. An example is when a company or industry secures a financial advantage by lobbying government for payments, like subsidies, or concessions, like lower taxes. Rent seeking undermines competition and productivity; if profitable, others may also do it, diverting resources that could be used to grow an economy's total wealth.

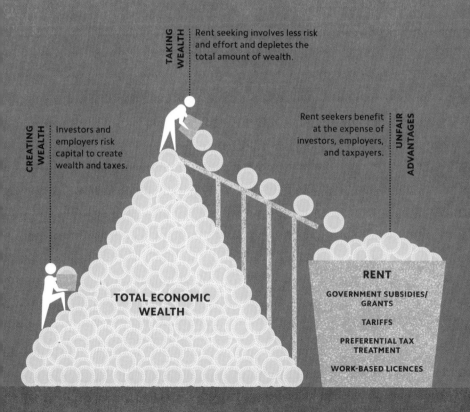

TAKING WEALTH
Rent seeking involves less risk and effort and depletes the total amount of wealth.

CREATING WEALTH
Investors and employers risk capital to create wealth and taxes.

UNFAIR ADVANTAGES
Rent seekers benefit at the expense of investors, employers, and taxpayers.

TOTAL ECONOMIC WEALTH

RENT
GOVERNMENT SUBSIDIES/ GRANTS

TARIFFS

PREFERENTIAL TAX TREATMENT

WORK-BASED LICENCES

THE VALUE OF IDEAS

Not all property is physical – ideas, too, need to be protected. Intellectual property (IP) gives a creator the right to make money from, or be credited for, a piece of intellectual labour, such as an invention or an artistic or literary work. In economic terms, IP grants a limited monopoly over the work for a period of time. Intellectual property rights deter people from copying or stealing works, and provide an incentive to produce new creations. The degree and scope of rights vary according to the class of intellectual property in question.

Trademark
A trademark protects a design, brand, or symbol that identifies a product as coming from a particular producer, and bars other companies from using or copying it.

Design rights
Design rights protect the look of a two- or three-dimensional article, including its shape, surface, colour, or decoration.

Non-fungible token (NFT)
An NFT is a digital record that denotes ownership of an asset, such as an artwork. Intellectual property rules still apply to the asset, but it is technology that ensures the token cannot be copied or replaced by another without permission – it is "non-fungible".

Trade secret
Trade secrets prevent confidential information, such as formulae or recipes, from being sold or used without permission.

Patent
A patent gives an inventor the legal right to prevent others from making or distributing their invention, or control how it is used. In return, the patent owner must disclose technical information about the invention in the patent document.

IP

Database rights
The contents of a database may qualify for protection if a significant investment was made in collating the data.

Copyright
The expression of new ideas is protected in law by copyright, which prohibits others from distributing or copying a work over a set period. Copyright is used by authors, artists, and filmmakers to protect their original creations.

> "Innovation is the commercial or industrial application of something new."
> Joseph Schumpeter

NEW IDEAS DRIVE GROWTH

In economics, innovation refers not just to a new idea, discovery, or invention, but is also about putting these to commercial use. This definition was first coined in 1943 by Joseph Schumpeter. Innovation is not limited to creating new products; it can also involve new ways of doing business or finding new markets for existing products. Together with entrepreneurship, innovation fuels new business activity, which in turn increases profits and economic growth – regarded by Schumpeter as the key to a successful capitalist economy.

The term "creative destruction" was popularized by Joseph Schumpeter in 1942. He used it to describe the way that new ideas or products continually tear down old ones in the market. In his analysis, this process underpins growth in the economy and is an essential driving force of capitalism. Success in an industry leads to profits so new entrepreneurs look at ways to capture some of those profits. As they do so, they tend to destroy the established companies, ideas, or products by creating new ones.

MAKING WAY FOR THE NEW

Small increments of innovation improve the offering to an existing market.

CHANGING THE PLAYING FIELD

The term "disruptive technology" was coined in 1995 for a particular type of innovation that opens up new markets and displaces existing providers. Disruptive technology initially offers worse performance than rivals, based on traditional criteria, but it soon appeals to more consumers, often due to lower prices or new functionality. For example, CD producers were focused on improving sound quality until MP3 redefined their industry. MP3 technology offered poorer sound quality but enabled lots of music to be stored on a portable device.

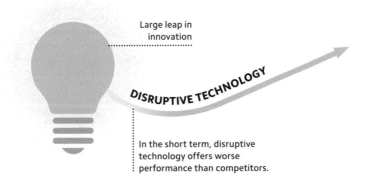

Large leap in innovation

In the short term, disruptive technology offers worse performance than competitors.

Comparing costs
Digital information goods' marginal costs
stay low over time, whereas those of many
physical goods will rise once production
increases to supply new customers.

MORE COSTS LESS

Information goods are products or services whose value lies in
the information they contain. Increasingly, they are in a digital
format, including ebooks, music, films, software, games, apps,
and social media feeds. A particular feature of digital information
goods is their minimal marginal costs. This means it costs very little
(or near zero) to reproduce each additional copy and distribute it
online. Costs are loaded into creating the good or service; then,
average costs continue to fall as it is provided to more users.

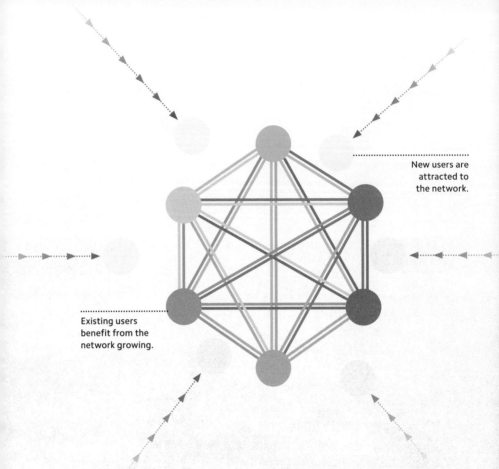

New users are
attracted to
the network.

Existing users
benefit from the
network growing.

USERS ATTRACT USERS

Network effects are benefits to a group of users – notably,
consumers of many information goods like software, games,
and social media. Direct network effects occur when each
new user increases the value of a network to users. For
example, as more people post on a social media platform its
content gets richer, attracting even more subscribers. When
enough people see an information good as worth more than
it costs them to obtain, the network expands rapidly due to
this effect – the business can then grow dramatically in scale.

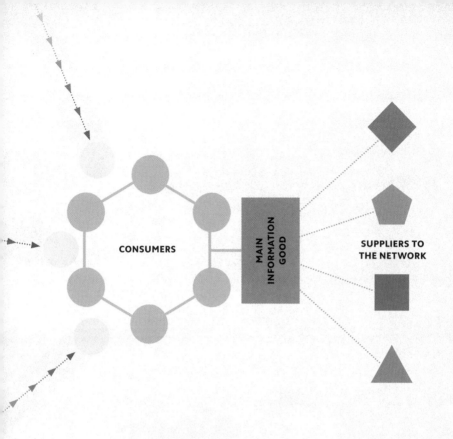

CONSUMERS

MAIN INFORMATION GOOD

SUPPLIERS TO THE NETWORK

USERS DRIVE QUALITY

An expanding network can indirectly generate benefits for itself; this effect often occurs with information goods. More consumer demand for a product or service prompts the supplier to make it more attractive (in order to grow its market share and pricing power), which benefits existing consumers. For example, an increase in streaming video customers may lead to more, higher quality shows. Third parties may also develop complementary products, like voice messaging on a gaming platform. These improve consumers' experiences and further boost demand.

INTERN
TRADE

ATIONAL

We live in an interconnected world, where all national economies interact with a global economy. Almost all countries trade with one another and so must manage complex factors, from having the right exchange rate to figuring out which goods and services to produce for export and which to import. Some countries raise barriers to protect their home markets, but economists usually find that this imposes undesirable costs on domestic consumers and that free, open trade is better for all parties. International trade is managed by supranational bodies, like the World Trade Organization (WTO), according to rules that have evolved to make this trade possible.

OPEN FOR BUSINESS

Free-trade policy allows goods and services from certain places to enter a country without restrictions. Countries may make bilateral free-trade agreements (between two parties) or join free-trade areas, where trade between partners is unrestricted, but trade from outside is regulated. Under free-trade agreements, a government should not subsidize any of its exporting industries because this gives an unfair advantage over foreign producers. Although less efficient domestic industries may suffer at the hands of foreign rivals, the aim of free trade is to ensure the most cost-effective supply of goods and services for consumers.

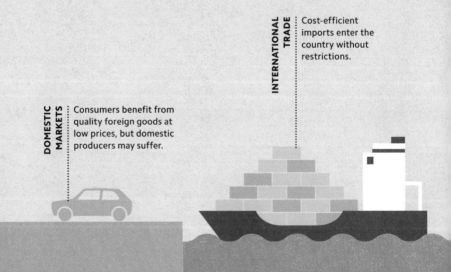

INTERNATIONAL TRADE
Cost-efficient imports enter the country without restrictions.

DOMESTIC MARKETS
Consumers benefit from quality foreign goods at low prices, but domestic producers may suffer.

(MOSTLY) CLOSED TO BUSINESS

The opposite of free trade, protectionism is when governments impose restrictions on goods and services entering their country. Quotas restrict how much can be brought in, and tariffs make imports more expensive. These policies protect domestic industries from foreign competition, and stop capital (productive resources) from leaving the country. Protectionism hopes to prevent unemployment and support fledgling industries, but it can lead to higher prices and inefficient industries. If all countries practised protectionism, world trade would decline and a global economic slump could result.

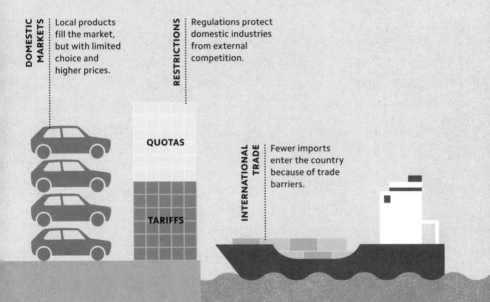

DOMESTIC MARKETS
Local products fill the market, but with limited choice and higher prices.

RESTRICTIONS
Regulations protect domestic industries from external competition.

QUOTAS

INTERNATIONAL TRADE
Fewer imports enter the country because of trade barriers.

TARIFFS

TRADE PARTNERSHIPS

Multilateral trade is when three or more countries agree to lower barriers like tariffs and quotas so they can trade more freely and, importantly, on the same terms. Its proponents say the benefits include cheaper imports, a more stable and transparent trading system due to standardized procedures, increased trade for all parties, and a stronger, more open global economy. In particular, multilateralism can level the playing field for smaller and emerging economies. One example of a regional multilateral deal is the United States–Mexico–Canada Agreement (USMCA).

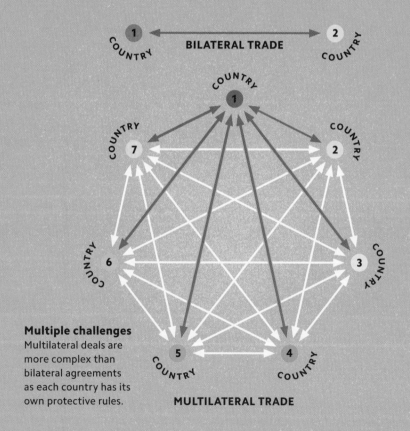

BILATERAL TRADE

Multiple challenges
Multilateral deals are more complex than bilateral agreements as each country has its own protective rules.

MULTILATERAL TRADE

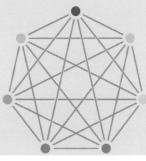

WTO

TRANSPARENCY

OPENNESS

IMPARTIALITY AND CONSENSUS

EFFECTIVENESS AND RELEVANCE

COHERENCE

THE DEVELOPMENT DIMENSION

REGULATING TRADE

Rules of trade exist to facilitate and support trade agreements within an alliance. The World Trade Organization (WTO) regulates global multilateral trading (see opposite) between more than 160 members. As well as creating and enforcing rules of trade, it acts as mediator should conflicts arise. The WTO operates on six principles that promote fairness: transparency, openness, impartiality and consensus, effectiveness and relevance, coherence, and the development dimension (which looks at how developing countries can be part of the global economy).

FREE TRADE... FOR SOME

CUSTOMS UNION

A customs union is where member states agree to reduce or abolish the trade barriers (such as tariffs and quotas) between them. The customs union levies a common external tariff on all trade goods entering it, but once inside goods may be traded without further tariffs. Customs unions increase trade flows between members, allow less efficient industries to survive, and increase members' bargaining power in trade deals with non-members. The European Union is the world's largest customs union.

No or low tariffs
Tariffs on goods traded between members are reduced or abolished.

No checks
Barriers to trade, such as border checks on goods, are removed.

Common external tariff
A single tariff applies to goods entering the customs union – this revenue is distributed between members.

Common trade deals
The customs union negotiates free trade deals with non-member countries on behalf of all its members.

TRADE PARTNERS

Two countries of equal size will trade four times more than two similar-sized countries twice as far apart.

LIKE ATTRACTS LIKE

To understand trade between countries, economists often use the gravity model of trade, suggested by Jan Tinbergen in 1962. It proposes that trade works like Newton's theory of gravity: the amount of trade between two countries will vary according to their mass – the size of their GDPs (see p.38) – but also to the distance between them. The bigger the two countries are, and the closer they are, the more they will trade. Closeness between countries refers not just to physical distance but also cultural preferences and development stage.

Global balance
Every export is an import into
another country, so the world's
balance of trade adds up to zero.

EVERYTHING ADDS UP

When a country exports goods or services, it receives a
payment, and when it imports them, it makes a payment.
A country's balance of trade is the difference between the value
of its exports and of its imports over a period of time. Countries
with a trade deficit must cover the difference by borrowing
money or allowing foreign investment, while those with a trade
surplus can lend money. However, whether a country's trade
balance is positive (surplus) or negative (deficit) is not necessarily
"good" or "bad" and does not reveal the health of its economy.

Trade deficit
When a country's imports
exceed its exports, it has a
negative trade balance.

Trade surplus
When a country's exports
exceed its imports, it has a
positive trade balance.

Fixed exchange rate
If a country pegs its currency to the value of another, its economy becomes more stable and is more attractive to foreign investment.

MONETARY UNION
A fixed exchange rate with some countries and a free flow of capital from others means foregoing monetary independence.

FINANCIALLY CLOSED SYSTEMS
If a country fixes its currency and also has monetary independence then it cannot have free-flowing capital.

Free flow of capital
A country can allow the free flow of capital with no fixed exchange rate from some or all other countries.

FLOATING EXCHANGE RATES
If a country has a free flow of capital and monetary independence, then the exchange rate cannot be fixed.

Independent monetary policy
The freedom for a country's central bank to control its supply of money enables it to respond to events.

INTERNATIONAL TRADE-OFFS

Economic theory suggests that when a country is deciding its international monetary policy (how it will interact with investment from other nations), it faces a trilemma – three mutually incompatible options. If two options are chosen, the third can never be realized. The three choices are a fixed exchange rate, a free flow of capital, or an independent monetary policy. Most countries choose a free flow of capital and monetary independence, sacrificing a fixed exchange rate.

WHO DOES IT BEST?

Absolute advantage is the ability of one country, region, business, or even individual to produce something more efficiently than another. In particular, it describes how one country can produce a particular good or service at a lower cost – perhaps by making more per hour or more for a given quantity of inputs. The idea was first introduced by Adam Smith in 1776 to explain how countries can grow richer through trade by concentrating on products which they can produce more efficiently than others.

COUNTRY 1

COUNTRY 2

Country 2 can make two cars and six bicycles, whereas, Country 1 can only make one car and four bicycles in the same time frame.

Country 2 has an absolute advantage over Country 1 in making both cars and bicycles. That means Country 1 should buy those items from Country 2 and look for other products to make.

Country 1 has a comparative advantage in bicycles as the opportunity cost to make one is a quarter of a car. (For Country 2, it is higher, at a third of a car.)

COUNTRY 1

**OPPORTUNITY
COST OF 1 CAR = 4 BIKES**

**OPPORTUNITY
COST OF 1 BIKE = ¹/₄ CAR**

COUNTRY 2

**OPPORTUNITY
COST OF 1 CAR = 3 BIKES**

**OPPORTUNITY
COST OF 1 BIKE = ¹/₃ CAR**

Country 2 has a comparative advantage in cars as the opportunity cost to make one is three bicycles. (For Country 2, it is higher, at four bicycles.)

WHO DOES WHAT BEST?

Comparative advantage is about the most efficient use of someone's resources, not who does something the best. A country or company has the comparative advantage when it focuses on its strengths and minimizes its opportunity costs (see p.80). This means not missing out on better ways to put its resources, time, and skills to work. The idea was developed by David Ricardo in the 1800s to explain why countries benefit from specializing and trading even when they have no absolute advantage.

WHY COUNTRIES SPECIALIZE

Traditional theories of free trade suggest that countries trade because a trading partner has an inherent advantage in creating a particular product, such as a cheap labour force or natural resources. Yet much of the world's trade is between similar countries. New trade theory (NTT) was devised in the 1970s to explain this. It showed that, by specializing in a particular niche, each country can achieve economies of scale. Meanwhile, its trading partner can do the same in another niche so both countries benefit. These economies of scale can help particular brands to dominate in a global market.

Economies of scale
Two countries might be equally able to produce both cars and bicycles, but economies of scale mean that they benefit by specializing in one and importing the other.

Country A exports cars at a lower price than Country B could produce them.

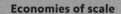

COUNTRY A
Country A achieves economies of scale in car production by selling to markets in two countries.

COUNTRY B
Country B achieves economies of scale in bicycle production by selling to markets in two countries.

Country B exports bicycles at a lower price than Country A could produce them.

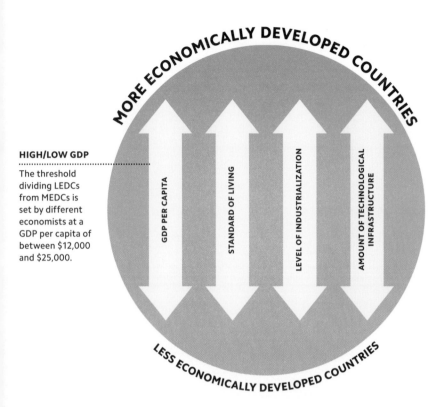

MORE ECONOMICALLY DEVELOPED COUNTRIES

HIGH/LOW GDP

The threshold
dividing LEDCs
from MEDCs is
set by different
economists at a
GDP per capita of
between $12,000
and $25,000.

GDP PER CAPITA

STANDARD OF LIVING

LEVEL OF INDUSTRIALIZATION

AMOUNT OF TECHNOLOGICAL
INFRASTRUCTURE

LESS ECONOMICALLY DEVELOPED COUNTRIES

COMPARING ECONOMIES

Countries have different levels of economic development,
which is measured by criteria such as Gross Domestic Product
(GDP; see p.38) per capita/person. Countries scoring lower on
these criteria are referred to as Less Economically Developed
Countries (LEDCs), and are concentrated in the southern
hemisphere; those with a higher score are termed More
Economically Developed Countries (MEDCs). One step in
economic development often leads to another – for example,
industrialization tends to increase a country's GDP, which
in turn improves the standard of living.

"The purpose of [aid] must be creating the conditions where it's no longer needed."
Barack Obama

GROWTH
Stronger growth and investment in development projects follows debt cancellation.

DEBT
A high debt burden acts as a drag on investment and growth.

DEBT RELIEF
Debt cancellation releases money for debtor nations to invest in growth.

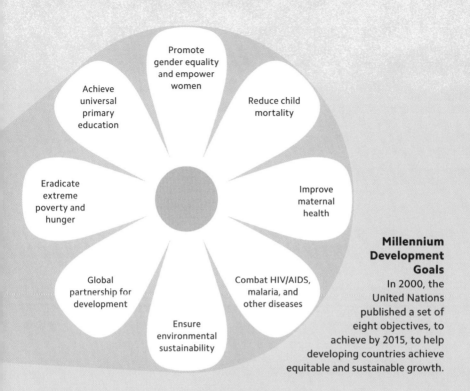

Millennium Development Goals
In 2000, the United Nations published a set of eight objectives, to achieve by 2015, to help developing countries achieve equitable and sustainable growth.

The petals of the diagram read:

- Promote gender equality and empower women
- Achieve universal primary education
- Reduce child mortality
- Eradicate extreme poverty and hunger
- Improve maternal health
- Global partnership for development
- Combat HIV/AIDS, malaria, and other diseases
- Ensure environmental sustainability

CANCELLING DEBT

Developing countries reportedly owe more than US$10 trillion in external debt. Repaying this level of debt starves poorer nations of money to invest in critical infrastructure and services and to support new industries. As a result, economic growth may stall, in turn increasing their risk of defaulting on debts. To avoid this, creditor nations and institutions establish debt relief programmes to reduce or reschedule payments, or to cancel some or all of the debt. Debtor (borrower) nations then have more to invest in vital development projects.

VALUING CURRENCIES

Currency is essentially the money that is exchanged for goods and services. Currencies are issued by national or supranational central banks. The exchange rate is the value of one currency compared with another – how much of one it costs to buy a particular amount of another. Most countries have free-floating currencies, meaning their value varies continually against others. But some are managed or even permanently fixed against another. Factors affecting floating exchange rates include a country's political stability, its current account (the balance of its exports and imports), inflation, and interest rates.

Appreciation
When one currency gains value, it is said to appreciate. This could be due to a fall in the cost of the country's imports or a rise in interest rates, which encourages investment.

Depreciation
When one currency loses value, it is said to depreciate. This could be due to a sudden drop in price of the country's major export or a rise in inflation.

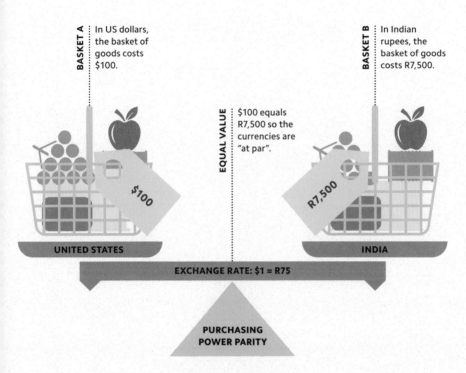

BASKET A: In US dollars, the basket of goods costs $100.

BASKET B: In Indian rupees, the basket of goods costs R7,500.

EQUAL VALUE: $100 equals R7,500 so the currencies are "at par".

$100

R7,500

UNITED STATES

INDIA

EXCHANGE RATE: $1 = R75

PURCHASING POWER PARITY

Comparing economies
with different currencies is
a challenge. One approach
is purchasing power parity (PPP).
Whereas the market exchange rate
expresses how much of one currency buys
another, the PPP exchange rate conveys how
much of each currency buys a comparable basket
of goods. If those costs in two countries are the same
when converted to the other's currency, then the currencies
are "at par". A wide range of goods is needed for a meaningful
result because prices can vary due to local variations such as taxes.

COMPARING CURRENCIES

New money
Full currency unions issue
their own banknotes and
coins. They often have a
central bank to control
their monetary policy.

In a currency union, two or more
countries agree to share a common
currency or fix the exchange rates between
their currencies. Currency unions eliminate the
risk of sharp exchange rate swings, which increases
the members' competitiveness in global trade. They
also remove the risks and costs of currency fluctuations
when doing business within the union. However,
economic shocks may affect member states
differently, and as individual states can no longer
use exchange rate adjustments to respond, some
may suffer disproportionately. The largest
currency union is the EU's Eurozone,
with 19 member states.

ONE COIN TO PAY THEM ALL

ONE CURRENCY FOR ALL

High labour mobility
Ideally, movement of labour within the OCA is flexible and visa free.

Capital mobility
Money and investment should be allowed to flow freely between members.

Shared risk
Members can transfer funds from regions with stronger economies to those facing difficulties.

Economic similarities
The more similar key factors like income distribution and GDP, the lower the risk of asymmetric shocks.

OCA

An optimum currency area (OCA) comprises several countries whose economies are sufficiently closely aligned that a single currency will maximize economic stability and growth. In OCA theory, certain factors are needed to gain the most benefit: for example, flexible labour and capital markets allow countries to make economic adjustments to cope with economic crises, instead of manipulating exchange rates. A currency union is less beneficial to countries with dissimilar economies – they are more liable to asymmetric shocks (sudden economic changes affecting only some), and may disagree on key trade and fiscal policies.

UNDERS
FINANC

TANDING
E

Money is vital to the workings of the modern economy, and finance is how that money, in its various forms, is managed. In a developed economy, the public sector, business, and individuals all require a trusted financial system. For a firm that needs to invest, the financial system provides the money they need and helps them deal with the problem of costs being incurred before revenues arrive. For individuals, it enables them to borrow to fund purchases and also provides somewhere to invest their surplus money for future growth. Savings, investments, and lending would not be possible without all the different kinds of finance available, from simple loans to complex financial instruments.

Liquidity is the measure of how easily an asset can be converted into cash – the most "liquid" asset. Bonds (see pp.144–145) and shares (see p.146) are also liquid since they can be traded for cash quickly: it is easy to define their value and there is a thriving market for them. Physical items such as property or art tend to be "illiquid" (less liquid) as it usually takes longer to find a buyer and agree a price. Businesses measure their liquidity to ensure they can access enough cash to cover expenses and unexpected costs.

CASH FLOWS FASTEST

"Liquidity is oxygen for a financial system."
Ruth Porat

Fiat money gives central banks and governments more control when it comes to managing economic variables – for example in a recession, a central bank can inject money into the economy by printing more. This means that fiat money is at risk of inflation.

Cryptocurrencies, such as Bitcoin, do not rely on banks or governments to enforce trust, or on intermediaries (for example PayPal or Visa) to process transactions. Because they are decentralized, they are also safe from a crash caused by a single point of failure.

FIAT MONEY

CRYPTOCURRENCY

OLD AND NEW MONEY

Fiat money is a government-issued currency, such as the pound, euro, and dollar. It has no intrinsic value – it is not based on an underlying commodity, but on trust – and its supply is regulated by centralized banks (see pp.58–59). It can be physical (as in bank notes) or digital (in a bank account) and transactions are linked to identities. Cryptocurrencies are purely digital, unregulated, and allow anonymous transactions. Their value comes from the blockchain – a decentralized database that processes and verifies all transactions – which offers security and transparency. Most cryptocurrencies have a limited supply, helping them to retain their value.

TRADING PLACES

Financial markets are physical and virtual arenas around the world where financial assets such as bonds, shares, currencies, or raw materials are bought and sold. They connect lenders with surplus money to borrowers who need it, for rewards reflecting the risks involved. Some markets offer highly liquid assets (see p.138) – money market investments (popular with banks and governments) typically have short durations of up to one year. Others, such as bond markets, may be used for long-term investment or saving. Businesses use markets to sell shares to investors to raise capital, and may purchase derivatives, based on the value of materials used in production, as a way of managing risk. Money also circulates via intermediaries such as banks, which create pools of capital and charge fees to investors. Not all trades are regulated – currency and derivatives trades often happen over the counter or directly between parties. Overall, financial markets let money flow where it is most needed, helping the global economy to function.

LENDERS

SAVERS

INVESTORS

KEY FINANCIAL MARKETS

Money markets
Here, low-risk, short-term debt products that are almost like cash are traded.

Bond markets
These offer longer-term, fixed-interest debt-based investments (see pp.144–145).

Stock markets
These are for trading shares – assets that confer company ownership (see p.146).

Foreign exchange markets
The foreign exchange is a global network of markets that deal in foreign currencies.

Commodities markets
Raw materials such as gold, oil, or wheat are traded as physical assets on these markets.

Derivatives markets
Here, investors can guard against or profit from future changes in asset prices (see p.147).

BORROWERS

GOVERNMENTS

BUSINESSES

INDIVIDUALS

INTERMEDIARIES

BANKS

PENSION FUNDS

INVESTMENT FUNDS

BROKERS

IDIOSYNCRATIC RISK

Events such as these can be managed by investing across different sectors.

SYSTEMATIC RISK

These kinds of events can negatively impact an entire stock, bond, or other financial market.

INTEREST RATE CHANGE

INFLATION

RECESSION

EXCHANGE RATE DECLINE

WAR

LOW LIQUIDITY

REGULATORY CHANGE

NEW ENTRANTS

SUPPLY PROBLEMS

INVESTOR

UNKNOWN RISKS

These arise from events that cannot be anticipated and planned for.

A RISKY BUSINESS

Financial risk is the chance of an event occurring that reduces the value of financial assets such as shares. It falls into two broad categories. Idiosyncratic risk affects shares in a specific industry or company. Therefore investors can protect against it by holding shares in diverse industries. Systematic risk affects a financial market or economy, so diversifying in this way will not help investors avoid it. However, the impact of systematic risk may be lessened by investing in different asset types (shares, bonds, gold, etc.), as these tend to react in varying ways.

STOCK MARKET CYCLES

When an economy is growing strongly and unemployment is low people feel confident that companies will make bigger profits and they want to invest more in shares (stocks), so demand pushes prices higher. Stock markets are measured by an index, like the FTSE-100, and if it rises by 20 per cent this is called a bull market – a period when share prices in that market are generally moving upwards. Eventually prices stop rising, often because the economy starts slowing down, and investors start selling to preserve gains or limit losses. As more sell, the market falls faster; if it drops by 20 per cent this is called a bear market – a generally downward phase.

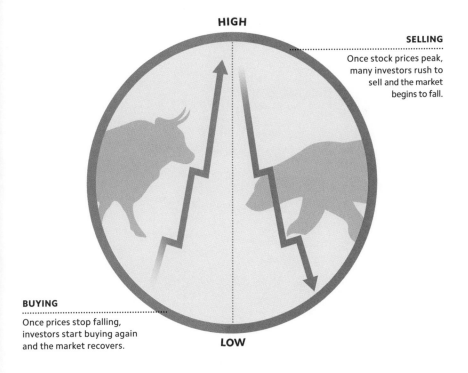

HIGH

SELLING
Once stock prices peak, many investors rush to sell and the market begins to fall.

BUYING
Once prices stop falling, investors start buying again and the market recovers.

LOW

BONDS = IOUs

Governments and businesses sell fixed-term loans called bonds when they need to borrow money (see p.151). Bonds are bought by investors, who receive interest payments during the term of the loan. When a bond matures, the investor is repaid the loan's face value (the amount they paid for it) by the seller. Investors can also sell their bonds to other investors before they mature. Although bonds tend to have a lower return than shares (see p.146) in the long term, they are seen as a less risky investment because repayment is guaranteed. Bonds are also more stable because they are backed by large organizations and are not dependent on market fluctuation.

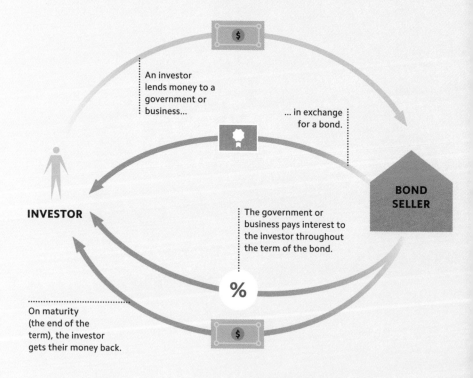

An investor lends money to a government or business...

... in exchange for a bond.

INVESTOR

BOND SELLER

The government or business pays interest to the investor throughout the term of the bond.

%

On maturity (the end of the term), the investor gets their money back.

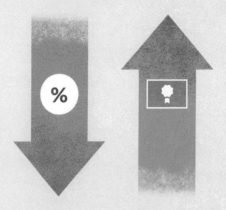

Ups and downs

Most bonds have a fixed interest rate, which makes them attractive to investors when market interest rates are falling. As a result, bond prices tend to rise as market interest rates go down (and vice versa).

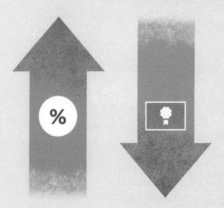

"Every portfolio benefits from bonds; they provide a cushion when the stock market hits a rough patch."

Suze Orman

ONE COMPANY, MANY OWNERS

Shares are small, equal pieces of a company's equity (the value of its assets) that can be bought or sold. The value of shares fluctuates with the value of the company, and if demand for shares is high, share prices will be high, too. Businesses sell shares to raise capital, and the investors who buy them become shareholders. Shareholders own a percentage of the business proportional to how many shares they own. This gives them the right to be involved in company decisions and, in some cases, to receive dividends – payouts from company profits.

Locked in

In a futures contract, the parties commit to buying or selling an asset for a fixed price on a set date. This allows them to lock in a price now for a future purchase.

THE RIGHT TO BUY

Option to buy

In an options contract, the buyer pays a small fee for the right – but, unlike futures, not the obligation – to buy an asset for a specified price on a set date.

A derivative is a contract based on the value of an underlying asset, such as a commodity or currency. The contract gives its owner the right to buy the asset for an agreed price on a specified date. If the value of the asset fluctuates, so too does the value of the derivative. Derivatives such as futures are often used to protect against risk, while options can be used to profit from changes to an asset's value by predicting how it will perform and trading the derivative.

THE PRICE IS RIGHT

The efficient market hypothesis (EMH) states that public and open markets use information efficiently, so market prices fairly reflect the true value of a company's stock. This means that it is not possible for investors to consistently identify under- or overvalued stocks by analysing past prices (weak-version EMH) and key business data like balance sheets (semi-strong EMH), or even using insider information (strong EMH). As a result, while an investor might get lucky, in the long run they will do no better than the market average.

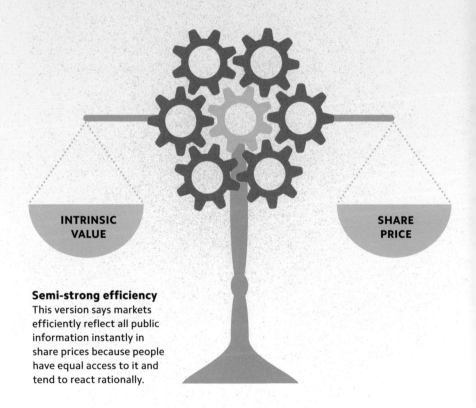

INTRINSIC VALUE

SHARE PRICE

Semi-strong efficiency
This version says markets efficiently reflect all public information instantly in share prices because people have equal access to it and tend to react rationally.

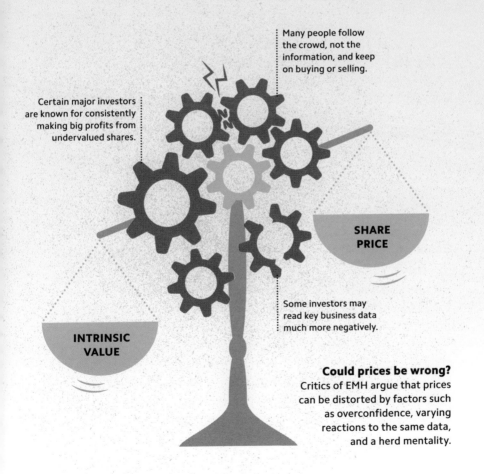

"In an efficient market...
the actual price of a security
will be a good estimate
of its intrinsic value."

Eugene F. Fama

Many people follow
the crowd, not the
information, and keep
on buying or selling.

Certain major investors
are known for consistently
making big profits from
undervalued shares.

SHARE
PRICE

Some investors may
read key business data
much more negatively.

INTRINSIC
VALUE

Could prices be wrong?
Critics of EMH argue that prices
can be distorted by factors such
as overconfidence, varying
reactions to the same data,
and a herd mentality.

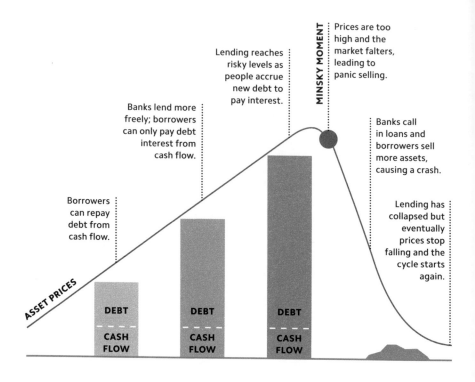

MINSKY MOMENT

Banks lend more freely; borrowers can only pay debt interest from cash flow.

Lending reaches risky levels as people accrue new debt to pay interest.

Prices are too high and the market falters, leading to panic selling.

Banks call in loans and borrowers sell more assets, causing a crash.

Borrowers can repay debt from cash flow.

Lending has collapsed but eventually prices stop falling and the cycle starts again.

ASSET PRICES

DEBT

CASH FLOW

DEBT

CASH FLOW

DEBT

CASH FLOW

GOOD TIMES BREED BAD TIMES

In the 1960s and 1970s, Hyman Minsky determined that financial markets, such as stock markets, are inherently unstable – that when they rise for too long, it leads to a crisis. While asset prices are rising, people feel confident they can repay their debts so they increase their borrowing to buy assets, which pushes prices higher. Eventually, both asset prices and debt levels become unsustainable. At that point – coined the "Minsky moment" in 1998 – prices will suddenly collapse as people panic sell in the hope of protecting their gains and repaying their debts.

RAISING CAPITAL

Businesses raise capital in two main ways: debt and equity.
In debt financing, a business sells debt instruments such as
bonds (see pp.144–145) to investors. The investors become
creditors to the business, and are guaranteed their initial
investment (the principal) back as well as regular interest
payments. Equity financing means selling an interest in the
business, such as shares (see p.146). Shareholders share
in the business's growth and may have voting rights on
business decisions, but there is no guaranteed repayment.

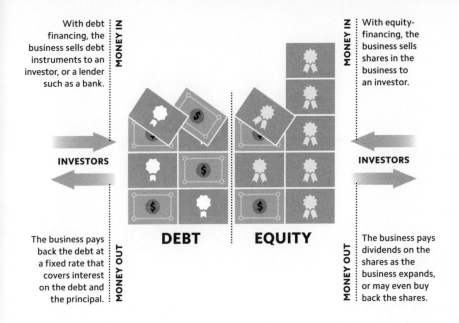

With debt
financing, the
business sells debt
instruments to an
investor, or a lender
such as a bank.

MONEY IN

MONEY IN

With equity-
financing, the
business sells
shares in the
business to
an investor.

INVESTORS

INVESTORS

The business pays
back the debt at
a fixed rate that
covers interest
on the debt and
the principal.

MONEY OUT

DEBT

EQUITY

MONEY OUT

The business pays
dividends on the
shares as the
business expands,
or may even buy
back the shares.

Money paid in the future is worth less than the same amount paid today, which can start earning interest now. To work out the present value of a future amount, "discount" it by the interest rate it could have earned. For example, if interest rates are 10 per cent, $100 paid in a year would be worth about $91 today ($100 divided by $110). Net present value (NPV) shows the difference between future earnings and future costs, discounted to today's value. It helps firms assess potential investments; a positive NPV indicates profitability.

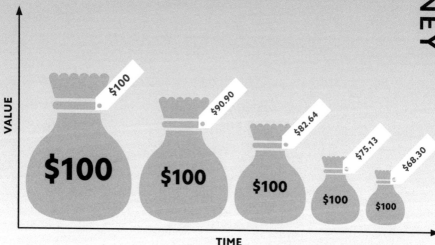

VALUE

TIME

$100 · $90.90 · $82.64 · $75.13 · $68.30

Time value
If interest rates were
10 per cent, $100 paid in
four years would only be
worth around $68 today.

"Simply stated, the value of a business today is the sum of all the money it will make in the future."
Peter Thiel

INVESTING FOR GROWTH

Venture capital (VC) is money and expertise that helps start-up businesses develop and grow quickly – provided by specialist VC firms, fund managers, and wealthy individuals with relevant experience. In exchange, investors take equity (a share) in the business and, often, a decision-making role. VC investors carefully select businesses in sectors with potential for rapid or extraordinary growth. They aim to exit after a few years by selling their equity and realizing exceptional gains. Until then, they often provide VC in stages to support specified goals.

Starting small
Early VC input might focus on refining the product or team.

Growing rapidly
Later-stage VC activity may help the business break a major new market or scale up production.

FOR SALE

NEW TO MARKET

Founders and early investors might decide to keep enough shares so they can stay in control of the company.

SHARE MAJORITY

An IPO valuation takes into account company finances, growth potential, market demand, and how similar companies have been valued.

VALUATION

GOING PUBLIC

An initial public offering (IPO) is when a private company issues shares to the public to raise money for a major expansion. A key part of this process is valuing the company to decide on the initial share price. The IPO will see some of the company's total shares sold to the primary market – usually investment institutions, such as pension funds. Later, these shares can be traded freely on the stock market (secondary market). Early investors (those involved in the company start-up and initial growth) often use the IPO as an exit strategy, selling their shares to get the returns they wanted from their investment. Others choose to hold on to their shares as the business grows.

Step 5
Based on the numbers, the business decides whether to implement the solution/product.

Step 4
Quantitative analysis of risks and benefits is synthesized, to structure the specific financial solution or product.

Step 3
The costs of these risks/outcomes are calculated and analysed using statistical and mathematical modelling.

Step 2
Analysts examine the business need and consider a solution, including its potential risks/outcomes.

Step 1
Primary research identifies the business need – a goal or a problem.

FINDING FINANCIAL SOLUTIONS

Financial engineering involves the use of advanced mathematics, computer programming, statistics, and economics to structure financial solutions, including financial products, often using instruments like derivatives (see p.147). These solutions enable businesses to manage specific risks, increase efficiency, and make the best possible strategic decisions. Engineers arrive at them by designing models, then testing and evaluating their likely financial upsides and downsides. For this reason, financial engineering is sometimes called quantitative analysis.

INDEX

Page numbers in **bold** refer to main entries.

ACKNOWLEDGMENTS

DK would like to thank the following for their help with this book: Phil Gamble and Vanessa Hamilton for the illustrations; Bonnie Macleod for editorial assistance; Alexandra Beeden for proofreading; Helen Peters for the index; Senior Jacket Designer Suhita Dharamjit; Senior DTP Designer Harish Aggarwal; Senior Jackets Editorial Coordinator Priyanka Sharma.